GLASS BELLS

A. A. Trinidad, Jr.

Schiffer Publishing Ltd

4880 Lower Valley Road, Atglen, PA 19310 USA

Designed by Bonnie M. Hensley
Cover design by Bruce M. Waters
Type set in Shelley Allegro BT/Korinna BT

ISBN: 0-7643-1265-0
Printed in China
1 2 3 4

Published by Schiffer Publishing Ltd.
4880 Lower Valley Road
Atglen, PA 19310
Phone: (610) 593-1777; Fax: (610) 593-2002
E-mail: Schifferbk@aol.com
Please visit our web site catalog at **www.schifferbooks.com**

In Europe, Schiffer books are distributed by Bushwood Books
6 Marksbury Avenue
Kew Gardens
Surrey TW9 4JF England
Phone: 44 (0) 20 8392 8585
Fax: 44 (0) 20 8392 9876; E-mail: Bushwd@aol.com
Free postage in the UK. Europe: air mail at cost.

We are always looking for people to write books on new and related subjects. If you have an idea for a book,
please contact us at the Atglen, PA. address. This book may be purchased from the publisher. Include $3.95 for
shipping. Please try your bookstore first. You may write for a free catalog.

Dedication

*To my wife, Josephine; together we
started to explore the world of glass bells.*

Our first bell.

Contents

Acknowledgments ─────────────────

The contribution of information from many bell collectors, museums, and bell producers over many years has made this book possible. I am especially indebted to the many friends in the American Bell Association who have been a source of information and encouragement to write this book.

My thanks to my editor, Donna Baker, for giving me the benefit of her experience with the writing and production of her two books on bells.

Thanks also to Bruce Waters for the painstaking effort in photographing bells from the author's collection and to Jean Vong for the photographs of bells of Jeremy Spear.

─────────────────────

Introduction

Bells have been used as a means of communication and ornamentation in many cultures for over three thousand years. Some of the earliest bells were metal, crotal type bells, found in Persia. Pre-Columbian bells have been found as clay rattles, as well as copper and gold ornaments among the Mayas and the Aztecs. In the Book of Exodus, chap. 28, v. 33-35, the priest's robe is described as made with gold bells and pomegranates alternating on the hem of the robe.

Generally, bells have been made of metal, porcelain, wood, clay, and glass. Among collectors, you will find animal bells (horse, camel, elephant, cow), transportation bells (railroad, trolley, bicycle, ship), commemorative bells (anniversary, historic), church bells, fire bells, and school bells. Figural and figurine bells in brass, bronze, silver, porcelain, and glass are very popular.

This book focuses attention on glass bells, presenting them by country of origin, type of glass, and manufacturer when known. When the manufacturer is not known, the bells are presented as unknown or under a special grouping.

Prices for bells vary based on condition, age, number made, availability, and attractiveness to the collector. Therefore, for bells shown herein a range of values has been shown.

In recent years many bell producing companies have merged with other companies, or presently are in the process of merging, making it difficult to determine their current status. The attributions presented in this book are the latest the author has been able to determine.

Chapter One
The History of Glass Bells

Few glass bells are known from early centuries. In the Toledo Museum of Art, Toledo, Ohio, there is an eastern Mediterranean glass bottle from the fourth to the sixth century with three glass bells attached to the outside. These are the oldest glass bells known to the author.

An eastern Mediterranean free blown glass flask, from the fourth to sixth century, with three blue glass bells attached. 7-1/2" high.
Courtesy of the Toledo Museum of Art, Toledo, Ohio.

A few commemorative Belgian, Dutch, and German glass bells are known from the six-teenth century and there are Bohemian and Venetian glass bells from the seventeenth century.

A sixteenth century Dutch "drinkout" bell called Duc d'Alf's "Ringing Out" glass bell. This refers to the renunciation of King Philip II by the States General in the Utrecht in 1581, but also to the king's commander and regent in the Netherlands, the much hated Duke d'Alba (hence the word-play Duc d'Alf) and his soldiers. During a festive banquet to honor this occasion, guests gave a toast to the New Republic's prosperity with these bells, or "drinkouts." *Courtesy of AMSTERDAMS HISTORISCH MUSEUM.*

A clear glass bell with metal additions including a brass handle. Probably from the Netherlands, c. 1550-1600. *Courtesy of the Victoria & Albert Museum Picture Library, London, England.*

Opposite page
A glass bell made in Antwerp, Belgium around 1580. It carries three medallions with facial masks depicting Neptune, the Roman god of the sea. Alternating with the masks are three bosses studded with small turquoise. The solid baluster handle, flecked with gold, is supported by four loops. The clapper is missing. 3"d. x 6-1/2"h. *Courtesy of Jeremy N. Spear.*

A dark blue, clear glass German bell mounted with a chased silver handle and three external clappers. Eighteenth century. *Courtesy of the Victoria & Albert Museum Picture Library, London, England.*

European marriage cups, while not strictly bells, have bell shaped base cups and are collected by bell collectors.

A German marriage cup, *jungfrauenbecher,* without the top swivel cup, decorated in blue and gold with what appears to be a coat of arms and a date of 1594. From head to skirt the bell is 8-1/2" in height. *Courtesy of Adeline Keehan Hill.*

A marriage cup with the base and top swivel cup in clear glass overlaid in gold decoration. Gold lettering on the base cup reads "Happiness and Prosperity!" The base is 3-1/2"d. and the overall height is 10-1/4". $650-700.

Bell goblets, which have a glass bell attached to the bottom of the bowl in place of the stem, were made in the Netherlands and Germany in the seventeenth century. However, most glass bells available to collectors, primarily from Europe and the United States, are known from the mid-eighteenth century to the present time. While some glass bells were used to call servants at the end of the nineteenth century, most recent glass bells have been made primarily for decorative purposes, souvenirs, advertising, and for commemorating events.

References

Springer, L. Elsinore. *The Collector's Book of Bells.* New York: Crown Publishers, Inc., 1972.
_____. *That Vanishing Sound.* New York: Crown publishers, Inc., 1976.
Trinidad, A. A. Jr. "Glass Bells." *Antique Trader's Collector Magazine & Price Guide.* Vol. 6, no. 3 (March 1999): 7-12.

Chapter Two
General Information

Glass

Glass is a homogeneous material produced by heating together a silica, from sand, and a flux, usually soda or potash. Soda glass, containing 15 to 25 percent soda, is the earliest form of glass. It is also known as soda-lime glass because it contains about 10 to 15 percent lime. It was first used for making items wholly of glass over four thousand years ago. It is lighter, less resonant, and less lustrous than lead glass, and likely to be flawed by bubbles and color tints. Glass that contains at least 20 percent lead oxide is known as lead glass. It is relatively softer, heavier, and stronger than soda glass, and has a refractive index that provides brilliance when the surface is covered with cut polished facets. In modern times, this type of glass was first used by George Ravenscroft in England about 1676.

Colored glass generally achieves its color by the use of various metallic oxides in the mixture fused in the process of making glass. Sometimes glass is colored by impurities in the basic ingredients. Color can also be achieved by embedding particles of colored material.

Flint glass is another name for a type of lead glass. It came into use during the seventeenth century in England when flint was used temporarily to replace sand as a source of silica. It has persisted since that time as an alternate name for lead glass.

Some bells are found in cased or plated glass, a glass that has been created by combining two or more layers of colored and clear glass. Cased glass is used primarily to emphasize a pattern that has been cut or engraved on the surface layer to reveal the clear or colored glass below. Flashed or stained glass has a very thin outer coating of colored glass made by dipping a clear glass object into a bath of colored glass. This technique has been used extensively on Bohemian glass bells where patterns are produced by engraving or etching the colored surface area.

Glass bells will be found in soda-lime and lead glass, the lead glass being used primarily for bells that have a cut or engraved design.

Forming the Bell

Glass bells are formed in several ways: free-blown, mold-blown, and mold-pressed. A free-blown bell is one in which the body has been shaped solely by inflating it with a blowpipe and shaping it with tools. Flameworking, sometimes called lampworking, is a form of free-blowing in which tubes of glass are heated in a flame or in gas-fueled torches and then manipulated to the desired shape. Mold-blown bells are made by blowing partly inflated hot glass into a mold; the glass then assumes the shape of the mold and any decoration that is on the mold. In mold-pressed bells, hot molten glass is forced into a multiple parts mold by means of a plunger to press the glass against the mold. In many blown bells the handle is formed separately and combined with the body of the bell while still hot or joined later by an adhesive. Some bells have the handle fitted into a sleeve at the upper end of the body of the bell and held there by plaster or other adhesive material.

Clappers and Attachments

Clappers produce a sound when striking a bell on the inside or outside. On glass bells, clappers are usually made of solid or hollow metal, glass, plastic, or wood. Metal clappers are known in silver, brass, bronze, iron, and lead. Most clappers are supported by a heavy or light metal chain or wire.

The method of attaching to the glass the chain or wire that holds a clapper varies and can sometimes be used to determine the approximate period of time during which the bell was produced. During the second half of the nineteenth century and the early twentieth century, most American cut glass bells supported a chain and two part hollow clapper by attaching the chain to a loop on a twisted iron wire embedded in the glass. From about the mid-1920s to around 1970, many bells had a hole formed or drilled at the base of the handle, the chain was inserted, and the hole filled with plaster. This method is common on better quality bells today. Since around 1970, many glass bells, worldwide, have the chain attached to a glass, metal, or plastic disk that is glued to the glass.

Large glass bells, made in two parts and joined by plaster, have a wire loop embedded in the plaster to hold the clapper, usually made of glass. This is typical of the wedding bells described in Chapter Eighteen.

Some bells have hollow handles, with the chain passing through the handle and attached to the top of the handle. Some American bells from the 1950s have a hollow handle with a cork inserted to hold the chain or wire. A few American bells from the twentieth century have two glass prongs holding the chain. Some companies had special clappers and attachments produced for their bells; these are described for specific bells in the following chapters.

Two part hollow ball metal clapper. Typical for American glass bells from the 1880s to the 1920s.

Decorating Methods

Glass bells have been decorated using four primary techniques (individually or in combination): cutting, engraving, etching, or painting. The base glass can be clear colorless, clear colored, colored opaque, or cased, also known as plated glass. When a bell is to be cut or engraved with a pattern, clear or cased lead glass is generally used. Because many cut glass patterns use deep cuts, glass blanks are made of thick glass. Thin glass blanks are used for shallower engraved patterns.

During the late nineteenth and early twentieth centuries, when a cut pattern was desired on a bell, the cutter started with a bell shaped glass blank on which a design was marked. Looking through the glass, the cutter applied the glass to rotating stone or metal wheels — of various sizes and shaped perimeters — while an abrasive suspended in water dripped on the wheel. The resulting completed pattern had a whitish gray color which had to be polished to produce a clear sparkling finish. Prior to the turn of the twentieth century, wooden wheels with rouge or putty powder were used for this polishing; after-

wards, a paste of pumice was used with cork or felt wheels to produce the required finish. To reduce labor costs, acid polishing using a combination of sulfuric and hydrofluoric acid was introduced at the end of the nineteenth century. Today, much of the cutting is done with diamond and bronze dust coated wheels.

Engraving of glass bells is sometimes combined with cutting on thick blanks. Engraving is done by applying a rotating copper wheel of various sizes to the glass. The wheels are fed with a mixture of oil or water and an abrasive. Sometimes the engraved pattern is left unpolished, leaving a gray or matte finish for contrast with the clear uncut areas.

Acid etching produces gray or frosted finishes, with a stencil used as a guide to produce the required design. In the early part of the twentieth century, needlepoint etching was sometimes used to produce a uniform design. The design was programmed into a machine that applied a needle to the revolving piece of glass.

Painting on bells is a common decoration used by itself or in combination with other decorating techniques. On some early twentieth century bells, the painted surface was not fired in the kiln to fix the paint, resulting in the bell losing some of the painted design over time.

A fifth technique deserves mention: carnival glass is glass that has been made iridescent by spraying a metallic salt on the surface of hot glass — prior to being reheated — to produce a characteristic metallic finish. It imitates the iridescent finish developed by Tiffany as Favrile Art Glass.

Identification

Very few glass bells can be identified by inscribed or etched signatures or trademarks. Many bells have been produced with paper labels that have since been removed. Generally, few American glass bells are signed; bells of some smaller art glass studios do show a signature. Some larger American glass houses that are producing or have produced bells used symbols. For example, Pairpoint uses a P in a diamond, while some Heisey bells have the familiar H in a diamond. The Imperial Glass Co. originally used its IG logo and, in its final years, an LIG and ALIG logos. Fenton started to use a signature in the 1970s.

The French glass houses producing higher quality bells, such as Lalique, Baccarat, Val St. Lambert, Daum, and Saint Louis, usually sign or etch a symbol on their glass bells.

The best way to identify the maker of glass bells is by studying the characteristics of the bells themselves, as most producers incorporated their own design features. For example, Heisey used a ruffle at the base of the handle on many of its bells. Of course, a paper label helps, if still on the bell. Labels can be found on many new American glass bells; most European glass companies use a paper label as well.

Chapter Three

American Cut Glass Bells:
By Their Handles You Will Know Them

When many of the books and catalogs on cut glass available to collectors are perused, very few cut glass *bells* are found to be illustrated. When looking for bells made of cased glass — colored on the outside surface with a pattern cut to expose the clear glass below — there are fewer still. Colored glass represented less than ten percent of all cut glass produced. Companies that cut bells also cut goblets in similar patterns; illustrations of these cut glass goblets are more prevalent and can therefore help to identify the company and the pattern of a bell. Only after seeing many American cut glass bells does it become apparent that most of the major cutting firms had their own distinctive patented patterns and some had one or more distinctive designs for cutting the handles of bells.

There were very few cut glass bells produced prior to the 1880s. In the homes of the more affluent in the late nineteenth and early twentieth centuries, cut glass bells to summon servants would be seen as part of table settings of rich cut glass. After the introduction of electricity in the 1890s, the availability of electric call bells gradually reduced the use of cut glass bells. After World War I, cut glass bells became primarily decorative.

The Brilliant Period of cut glass in the United States, from the time of the Centennial in 1876 to about 1915, was a period in which many fine cut glass bells were produced in geometric patterns using lead glass. Overlapping this period was the Flower Period, from about 1906 to the 1920s, during which cut and engraved flowers and other natural subjects appeared on bells. At about the same time, less expensive pressed pattern glass bells were being made in imitation of the more expensive cut glass patterns. A prime example is the Daisy and Button pressed glass pattern, produced by many companies, which copied the Russian pattern in cut glass first produced by T. G. Hawkes & Company in White Mills, Pennsylvania.

As described in Chapter One, a study of clappers used on bells helps to identify generally the period in which bells were produced. On most American cut glass bells from the Brilliant Period and the Flower Period, a chain supporting a clapper was attached to a loop in a twisted wire embedded in the glass. The Hawkes company is the only American cut glass company known by the author that rarely used the twisted wire attachment; that company, throughout its long history of producing bells, attached the chain to the glass primarily by inserting the chain in a hole in the glass and filling the hole with plaster.

Lead glass blanks used for cut glass were produced by many American companies, but primarily by the Corning Glass Works, C. Dorflinger & Sons, and the Union Glass Co. Other American glass companies producing blanks were H. C. Fry Glass Co., Libbey Glass Co., and Steuben Glass Co. Some blanks, particularly in colored glass and cased glass, came from European companies. Blanks specifically for bells can be attributed to the Dorflinger, Steuben, and Union companies.

Below is an alphabetical listing of American companies that produced cut glass bells, along with examples of some of the bells they made.

J. D. Bergen Company
Meriden, Connecticut, 1880-1922

The J. D. Bergen Co. produced many fine bells, primarily using blanks that were 5 1/4", 6", and 7 1/2" high. Bergen bells have a very distinctive pattern cut at the top of the handle. The top has sixteen radial miter cuts to form a star, and the circumference just below the top has a linear pattern of double crosses in a diamond.

Typical pattern for top of handle of Bergen bells. Sixteen radial miters form a star at the top surrounded by a pattern of double crosses in diamonds.

Two J. D. Bergen Co. cut glass bells in "Premier" pattern. 3"d. x 5-1/4"h. and 3-1/4"d. x 6"h., c. 1904. $300-450 ea.

A J. D. Bergen cut glass bell in the "Electric" pattern. 3"d. x 5-1/2"h., c. 1904. $300-400.

A J. D. Bergen cut glass bell in the "Dauntless" pattern. 3"d. x 5-1/2"h. $300-400.

A J. D. Bergen cut glass bell in the "Genoa" pattern. 3"d. x 5-1/2"h. $300-400.

A J. D. Bergen cut glass bell in a "Strawberry Diamond and Fan" pattern. 3-3/4"d. x 7-1/2"h. $650-700.

A. L. Blackmer Company
New Bedford, Massachusetts, 1894-1916

The Blackmer Company produced only a few bells, but these have very distinctive patterns.

An A. L. Blackmer Co. cut glass bell with an unusual handle in the "Crawford" pattern. 3"d. x 4-3/4"h. $425-475.

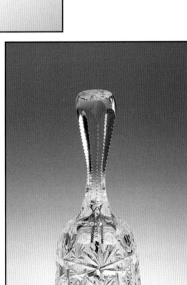

An A. L. Blackmer Co. glass bell cut with stars and a radial star on the flat top of the handle, in the "Aetna" pattern. 3-1/4"d. x 6"h., c.1900. $300-400.

Boston & Sandwich Glass Co.
Sandwich, Massachusetts, 1870-1887

The author is aware of three different colored bells cut with the "Ionic" pattern, a pattern illustrated on a decanter in an 1874 Boston & Sandwich catalog. The bells are known in a lime green, ruby, and blue colored glass cut to clear, but with different handles. Some Boston & Sandwich engraved glass bells are shown in Chapter Four.

A green cut to clear Boston & Sandwich glass bell in the "Ionic" pattern. 3-1/4"d. x 4-3/4"h., c. 1874. $500-600.

A red cut to clear Boston & Sandwich glass bell in the "Ionic" pattern. 3-1/4"d. x 4-3/4"h., c. 1874. $500-600. *Courtesy of Vernon and Jonni Jones.*

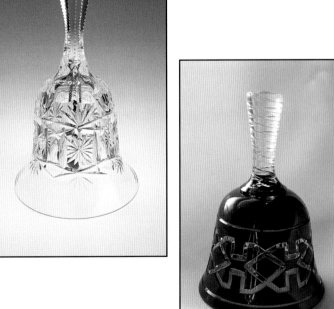

A blue cut to clear Boston & Sandwich glass bell in the "Ionic" pattern, with a twisted clear glass handle. 3-1/4"d. x 4-1/2"h., c. 1874. $500-600. *Courtesy of Vernon and Jonni Jones.*

T.B. Clark & Co.
Honesdale, Pennsylvania, 1884–1927

The T. B. Clark Company produced bells also with a very distinctive pattern cut at the top of the handle. The top has radial miters forming a star with a crosscut diamonds pattern encircling the side just below the top. Some Clark bells are known also to have used a blank similar to that used by their subsidiary company, the Maple City Glass Co.

A Clark bell in ruby cut to clear in their "Jewel" pattern. 3"d. x 5-1/2"h. c. 1896. $1,800-2,000. *Courtesy of Bob Hampton.*

A T. B. Clark & Co. cut glass bell in their "Jewel" pattern. 3"d. x 5-1/2"h., c. 1896. $400-500.

The cut pattern for the top of handle of some T. B. Clark bells: a radial miter star on top surrounded by crosscut diamonds.

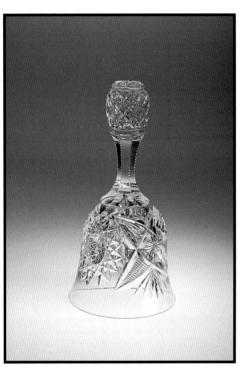

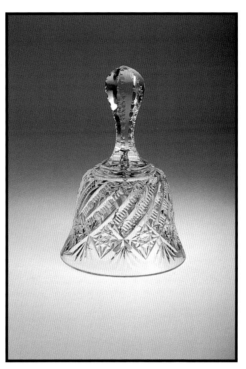

A T. B. Clark & Co. cut glass bell in their "A-E" pattern. 3"d. x 6"h., c. 1901. $450-500.

A T. B. Clark cut glass bell, with a different handle, in the "Orient" pattern, c. 1896. $300-400.

A T. B. Clark & Co. cut glass bell in a "Harvard" pattern. 3"d. x 5-3/4"h., c. 1905. The blank for this bell, with a handle different from the previous Clark bells, is the same as that used by Maple City Glass Co. (a Clark subsidiary) for their bells. $350-400.

C. Dorflinger & Sons
White Mills, Pennsylvania, 1865–1964

The Dorflinger company produced some of the finest cut glass bells in the United States at the end of the nineteenth century and beginning of the twentieth century. Their bells have three very distinctive designs cut on the tops of the handles. Two of these designs are prevalent. One has strawberry diamonds cut on the top and along the perimeter immediately below the top of the handle; the other shows radial miters cut on a relatively flat top of handle. The less prevalent design has raised buttons on a curved top of handle and the buttons are decorated with parts of the design cut on the body of the bell. Most of the bells have handles with six sides, but an occasional bell will have an eight-sided handle.

Dorflinger glass bells generally were produced from four different size molds with known finished heights of about 5 1/2", 6 1/2", 7 1/2", and 8 1/2".

A November 10, 1897 advertisement in *The Jewelers Circular* shows that Dorflinger cut glass bells in crystal and three colors: ruby, blue, and green. The price was noted as $1 and up!

A Dorflinger advertisement from the November 10, 1897 issue of *The Jewelers Circular.*

In the records on Dorflinger glass at the Corning Museum Rakow Library is a Lambert Dorflinger salesman's book from about 1895. This book lists thirteen bell patterns available. Their prices vary with the size of the bell and whether they are in crystal or colored (see chart below). Based on this listing and other known Dorflinger patterns on bells that are not listed in that book, over one hundred different Dorflinger bells may exist.

PATTERN		
Parisian	Oriental	S D & F
Sultana	Star & Diamond	Colonial
Dresden	Royal	Marlboro
American	Hob Diamond	
Belmont	Lorraine	
$	$	$
CRYSTAL		
L/S 7.50	6.00	3.50
S/S 6.00	5.00	3.00
COLORED		
L/S 8.00	7.00	4.50
S/S 7.00	6.00	4.00

The most prevalent of three cut designs for top of handle of Dorflinger cut glass bells. The top is cut in strawberry diamonds.

Three Dorflinger bells cut in the "Strawberry Diamond & Fan" pattern with prevalent handle, the left bell in green cut to clear, the center bell in clear glass, and the right bell in blue cut to clear. All 3-1/2"d. x 7-1/4"h., c. 1890. Clear bell $700-900; colored bells $2,000-2,200. Similar bells also exist 8-1/4" high.

Left: A smaller Dorflinger clear glass bell cut in the "Strawberry Diamond & Fan" pattern. 2-1/4"d. x 5-3/4"h. $400-600.

Right: A Dorflinger bell in ruby cut to clear in a different blank, but with the same prevalent strawberry diamond handle, in "Strawberry Diamond & Fan" pattern. 3-3/4"d. x 6-1/4"h. $1,900-2,100.

A smaller Dorflinger bell in green cut to clear "Strawberry Diamond & Fan" pattern. 3"d. x 5-1/2"h. $1,600-1,800.

A Dorflinger bell engraved with initials, leaves, and a date of October 13, 1893. The blank for this bell is probably the same as for the green cut to clear bell. Was this bell made for the Columbian Exposition of 1893 in Chicago, Illinois? 3"d. x 5-1/2"h. $300-350.

A Dorflinger bell cut in the "Marlboro" pattern. 3"d. x 5-1/2"h., c. 1900. $600-700.

A Dorflinger bell cut in the "Colonial" pattern. 3"d. x 5-1/2"h., c. 1896. $600-700.

Two Dorflinger bells cut in a common but unknown pattern, consisting of a hobstar, fan, and two triangles filled with cross-hatching alternating with a pair of fans. The bell on the left is 3-1/2"d. x 7-1/4"h.; the one on the right is 3-3/4"d. x 8"h. $700-900 ea.

A Dorflinger bell cut in the "Parisian" pattern. 4-1/2"d. x 6-1/2"h., c. 1886. $800-900. *Courtesy of Bob Hampton.*

Left: A Dorflinger bell in unknown pattern, hobstar and fans alternating with a row of diamonds filled with cross-hatching. 3-1/2"d. x 8-1/2"h. $800-1,000.

Right: A Dorflinger bell cut in the "Roxana" pattern with the star top of handle. 3"d. x 5-3/4"h., c. 1913. $500-600.

A second Dorflinger top of handle with twelve radial miters forming a star.

A Dorflinger bell in ruby cut to clear in a "Renaissance" pattern with the star top of handle. 3"d. x 5-3/4"h., c. 1910. $1,700-1,900.

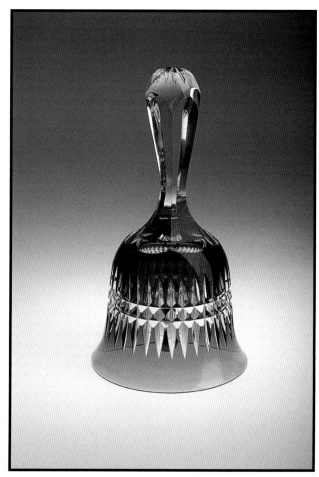

A third Dorflinger design for top of handle: raised buttons with parts of the design that are cut on the body of the bell.

A Dorflinger bell cut in a "Royal" pattern with the raised buttons top of handle that has eight sides instead of the usual six-sided handle. The cross-hatching and stars of the Royal pattern are cut into the buttons. 3-1/2"d. x 7-1/4"h., c. 1891. $900-1,000.

A Dorflinger ruby cut to clear bell in the "Royal" pattern. 3"d. x 5-3/4"h., c. 1891. $2,100-2,400.

Empire Cut Glass Co.
Flemington, New Jersey, 1904-1925

The Empire Cut Glass Co. produced very few bells. The only pattern the author has seen is their Henry pattern bell, made around 1910 on a clear blank.

An Empire Cut Glass Co. bell cut in the "Henry" pattern, an eight petal flower with pointed leaves. 2-3/4"d. x 6-3/4"h., c. 1910. $300-350.

H. C. Fry Glass Co.
Rochester, Pennsylvania, 1901-1954

The March 15, 1906 issue of the *Crockery and Glass Journal* pictures a cut glass replica of the Liberty Bell measuring 28" in height, including a metal handle, and having a bottom diameter of 24". The design includes a reproduction of the United States flag, the Great Shield of the United States, 24 point hobstars, and a simulated crack. The glass weighs sixty pounds. It is generally believed to have been exhibited at the 1905 Lewis & Clark Exposition in Portland, Oregon with some other very large Fry cut glass articles. It is the largest cut glass bell known to the author.

The bell without a handle is owned by Jim Miller, a cut glass collector, who showed a photograph of his bell in an article on Patriotic Motifs in Cut Glass published in the June/July 1999 issue of the *Glass Collector's Digest*.

The author is not aware of any other glass bell cut by Fry.

An H. C. Fry Glass Co. cut glass Liberty Bell believed to have been exhibited at the 1905 Lewis & Clark Exposition in Portland, Oregon. The original metal handle is missing. Original overall dimensions were 24"d. x 28"h. *Courtesy of the Miller Collection: Joe, Francis, and Jim Miller, Harrison, Arkansas.*

The March 15, 1906 issue of the *Crockery and Glass Journal* pictured the Fry Glass Liberty Bell.

T. G. Hawkes & Co.
Corning, New York, 1880-1962

The T. G. Hawkes company produced many fine glass bells during its eighty-two year history of production of cut glass articles. The company's production of engraved glass bells on thin glass is presented in Chapter Four. Like many other glass houses, Hawkes produced many fine goblets in known patterns similar to those on bells, and these help to identify the patterns on their many bells.

On all but a few Hawkes bells, the chain holding the clapper was attached to the glass by inserting the chain in a pre-formed or drilled hole and filling the hole with plaster. This is contrary to the clapper attachment method of embedding a twisted wire into the glass, used by other cut glass companies during the Brilliant Period and Flower Period of American cut glass. However, it is known that Hawkes salvaged broken stemware by converting some of them to bells — accomplishing this by drilling a hole and inserting the chain and plaster. A September 27, 1892 letter from Hawkes to Davis Collamore & Co. confirms this:

Your esteemed favor of the 22nd. inst. received. In regard to the bell sent on special order number 2, would say, that we use the bowls of broken hocks and clarets for these bells, as we have had before explained to you, but as we had none in stock cut Russian, we sent the nearest thing we had. We can cut a bell specially for you if you wish, but it would be considerably more expensive, as we only put these bells in at these prices to get rid of our broken hocks, etc. Please let us know if we shall do so, or shall we wait until we have some more broken hocks Russian? It may be some months before we do though.

Earlier than 1915, Hawkes used a special solid silver clapper produced by the Gorham Manufacturing Co. In a letter dated January 31, 1888 to Hawkes from W. H. Glenny & Co., a Hawkes distributor in Rochester, New York, Hawkes was requested to send bells with wooden clappers as the metal clappers broke the bells easily. One bell broke while simply showing to a customer. The Gorham clapper used on the broken bell was a very heavy, solid silver, dumbbell shaped clapper used on Hawkes bells from the 1880s to the early 1900s. Hawkes must have learned from this experience with broken bells, as some bells produced around the year 1900 are known with a wooden clapper. Around 1915, Hawkes bells appear with metal clappers in a shape similar to the earlier clappers, but weighing about half the weight of the original metal clappers.

Three Hawkes bells. Left to right: c. 1880s "Russian" pattern, c. 1900 "Marion" pattern, c. 1915 "Strawberry Diamond & Fan" pattern. See corresponding clappers in next photo.

Clappers for the three Hawkes bells. Left to right: c. 1880s large solid silver sinker type clapper, c. 1900 wooden clapper, c. 1915 smaller solid silver sinker type clapper. Hawkes learned from their experience with broken bells to use lighter clappers.

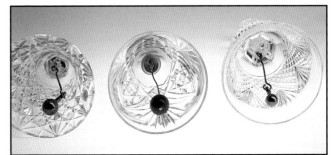

From about 1915 to the 1950s, the clapper used by Hawkes has a two-part, hollow metal ball attached to a chain. This is typical of clappers used by American firms during that period and before.

Three T. G. Hawkes bells, clear and colored cut to clear, in a "Strawberry Diamond & Fan" pattern. 3"d. x 5-1/2"h., c. 1915. Clear bell is signed HAWKES at base of handle. On all Hawkes bells, the chain holding the clappers is connected to the glass by inserting the chain in a drilled or pre-formed hole and filling it with plaster. See next photograph for special clapper for these bells. Clear bell $400-600. Colored bells $900-1,100.

A typical sinker shaped, silver clapper used on Hawkes bells from 1880s to about 1915. From 1915 to the 1950s, Hawkes used a two-part hollow metal clapper typically used by other companies.

A Hawkes bell cut in the "Russian" pattern with a large sinker type silver clapper. 2-3/4"d. x 5-1/4"h., c. 1880s. $500-700.

A Hawkes bell cut in the "Marion" pattern with a silver handle made by Gorham. The clapper is a round wooden ball used by Hawkes for several years because the earlier heavy solid silver clappers were breaking bells. The bell is signed HAWKES on the shoulder. 2-3/4"d. x 5-1/4"h., c. 1900. $400-600.

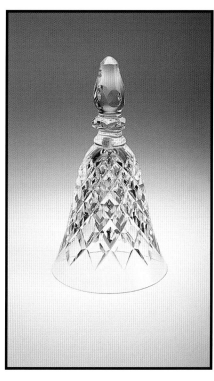

An original photograph of three Hawkes bells in patterns. Left to right: "Lace Hobnail," "Hobnail," and "Strawberry Diamond." 2-3/4"d. x 5-1/4"h., c. 1900.

A Hawkes bell cut in the "Delft Diamond" pattern, signed HAWKES on the shoulder of bell. Hollow metal two part clapper. 2-3/4"d. x 4-3/4"h., c. 1950s. $150-200.

A heavy Hawkes cut glass bell in an unknown pattern, a hobstar and fans alternating with double diamonds filled with cross-hatching. 3-1/2"d. x 6"h. $400-600.

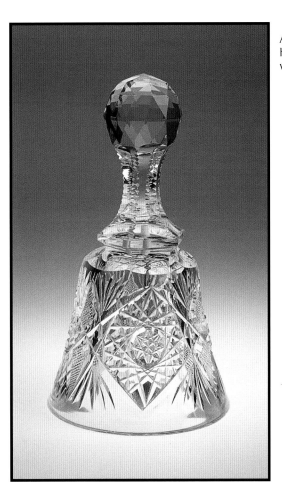

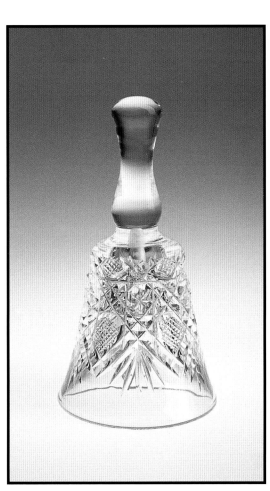

A heavy Hawkes cut glass bell in the "Kent" pattern. 3-1/2"d. x 6"h. $600-800.

A small cut glass bell in a "Harvard" pattern, attributed to Hawkes based on the attachment of the faceted crystal clapper. It is the smallest American cut glass bell known to the author. 1-1/2"d. x 3"h. $200-300.

J. Hoare & Co.
Corning, New York, 1853-1920

Hoare produced many fine bells. The handles typical of Hoare bells have six sides with notched corners and two or three horizontal miters.

J. Hoare & Co. cut glass bell in the "Monarch" pattern. Note the curved miters in the pattern at right hand side of the photograph in this variation of the "Monarch Pattern." 3"d. x 4-1/2"h., c. 1896. $400-600.

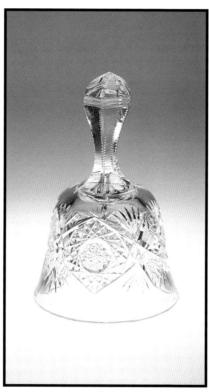

Another Hoare cut glass bell in the "Monarch" pattern. Note that in this variation of the "Monarch" pattern the curved miters have been replaced by a diamond shaped pattern. This variation can be seen in Hoare's 1911 catalog. 3"d. x 4-1/2"h. $400-600.

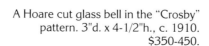

A Hoare cut glass bell in the "Crosby" pattern. 3"d. x 4-1/2"h., c. 1910. $350-450.

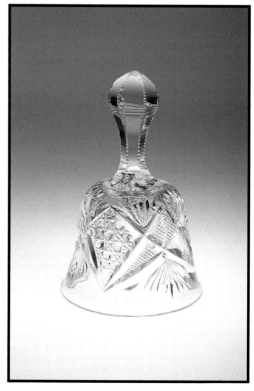

A Hoare cut glass bell in the "Delft" pattern. 3"d. x 4-1/2"h., c. 1910. $350-450.

A Hoare glass bell in a taller blank cut in the "Pluto" pattern. 3"d. x 5-1/2"h., c. 1910. $250-300.

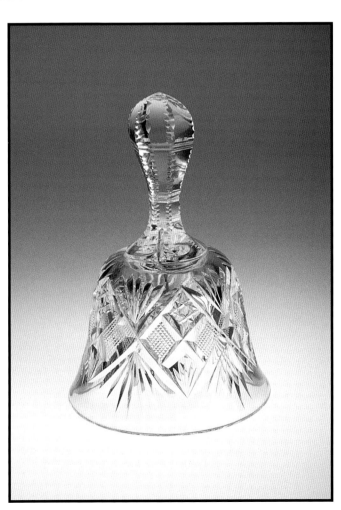

A Hoare cut glass bell in the "Tokio" pattern. 3"d. x 4-1/2"h., c. 1910. $350-450.

G. W. Huntley Co.
Chicago, Illinois, 1913

A 1913 catalog is known for the G. W. Huntley Co., a wholesale distributor, which shows a "Plaza" pattern on cut glass.

A G. W. Huntley Co. bell in the "Plaza" pattern. 3"d. x 4-1/2"h. $300-350. *Courtesy of Vernon and Jonni Jones.*

Libbey Glass Co.
Toledo, Ohio, 1880-1935

Libbey produced very few cut glass bells.

A Libbey Glass Co. glass bell cut in the "Corinthian" pattern. 3"d. x 5-1/2"h. $450-500.

Maple City Glass Co.
Honesdale, Pennsylvania, 1898-1927

The Maple City Glass Co. produced many fine bells with plain hexagonal handles. Maple City is believed to have been a subsidiary of T. B. Clark & Co., who sometimes used the same glass blank for bells as Maple City.

A Maple City Glass Co. glass bell cut in the "Baltic" pattern. 3"d. x 5-3/4"h., c. 1906. $350-400.

The multifaceted top of handle typical of Maple City Glass Co. bells.

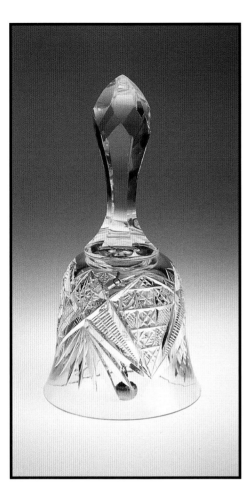

A Maple City glass bell cut in the "Texel" pattern. 3"d. x 5-3/4"h., c. 1909. $350-400.

A Maple City glass bell cut in the "Waldo" pattern. 3"d. x 5-3/4"h., c. 1911. $350-400.

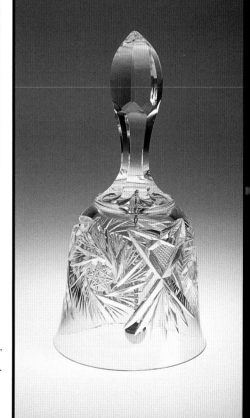

A Maple City glass bell cut in the "Kent" pattern. 3"d. x 5-3/4"h., c. 1911. $350-400.

Meriden Cut Glass Co.
Meriden, Connecticut, 1895-1923

The author has seen several bells that may be attributed to Meriden based on the star pattern that is common on some Meriden cut glass.

A bell believed by the author to be a Meriden Cut Glass Co. bell cut in an unknown pattern. The star pattern of this bell is a typical pattern found on Meriden cut glass articles. 3"d. x 5-3/4"h. $400-500.

Mount Washington Glass Co.
New Bedford, Massachusetts, 1869-1900

In the Pairpoint archives in the Rakow Library at the Corning Museum of Glass, there is a Book 1, with ware and prices, probably used between 1880 and 1885, with later additions in 1892. One cut glass bell is noted as pattern no. 60 (a Russian pattern), fluted with no fans

and having a knob handle. Several bells are noted in the Strawberry Diamond and Fan pattern also with a knob handle. No bells are illustrated, however.

John S. O'Connor
Hawley, Pennsylvania and Goshen, New York, 1890-1919

During the period in which John S. O'Connor worked for C. Dorflinger & Sons, he invented a special cutting wheel that enabled Dorflinger to cut distinctive patterns with curved miters. O'Connor left Dorflinger in 1890 to establish his own firm in Hawley, Pennsylvania. He later sold the Hawley factory to the Maple City Glass Co. as their second factory and opened a shop in Goshen, New York. O'Connor is well known for his Princess or Split Square pattern on cut glass.

A John S. O'Connor glass bell cut in the " Princess" or "Split Square" pattern patented on February 19, 1895. 3-3/4"d. x 7-1/2"h. $700-800.

Pairpoint Corporation
New Bedford, Massachusetts, 1900-1938

The Pairpoint Corporation produced few cut glass pattern bells and is better known for its blown bells produced after 1970 by a successor company. The company's cut glass bells usually have a solid silver ball clapper and silver chain.

A Pairpoint Corp. glass bell cut in a daisy design. The solid clapper and chain are made of silver. 2-3/4"d. x 5"h., c. 1930s. $200-250.

A Pairpoint glass bell cut in a crabapple design. This bell also has a solid silver clapper and chain. 3"d. x 6"h., c. 1920s. $300-350.

Pepi Herrmann Crystal
Gilford, New Hampshire, 1974-

Pepi Herrmann Crystal has produced some of the finest cut glass bells since the Brilliant Period of American cut glass. The output of cut glass bells has been limited by the number of glass blanks available primarily from Europe. The author is aware of at least eight different bell shapes in cut glass. Some bells have been produced in unique, one-of-a-kind patterns.

Two Pepi Herrmann Crystal bells cut in "Marc Patrick" pattern (left) and "Presidential" pattern (right). Note the uncut handles on these earlier bells. 3"d. x 6-3/4"h., c. 1980s. $110-130 ea.

Two Pepi Herrmann bells cut in "Exquisite" and "Bratislava" patterns. 3"d. x 6-3/4"h., 1989 and 1994 respectively. $130-150 ea.

Two Pepi Herrmann bells cut in "one of a kind" patterns in 1997. 3"d. x 6-3/4"h. $200+ ea.

Three Pepi Herrmann bells in cut patterns of "Comet" in 1996, "Vienna" in 1994, and "Daniela" in 1989. 3"d. x 6-3/4"h. $140-160 ea.

Three Pepi Herrmann bells cut in "one of a kind" patterns on a smaller blank in 1997. 2"d. x 3-3/4"h. $100+ ea.

Opposite page
Bottom right: Three Pepi Herrmann Crystal bells cut, left to right, in "Romance," "Andrea," and "Strawberry Diamond & Fan" patterns with cut handles. 3"d. x 6-3/4"h., made in 1989, 1994, and 1989 respectively. $130-150 ea.

Three Pepi Herrmann bells cut in "Spiral," "Star," and "Gothic" patterns in 1995. 1-3/4"d. x 4-1/2"h. $80-100 ea.

Three Pepi Herrmann bells cut in "Exquisite," "Marc Patrick," and "Jewel" patterns in 1995. 1-3/4"d. x 4-1/2"h. $80-100 ea.

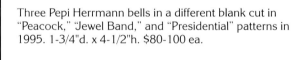

Three Pepi Herrmann bells in a different blank cut in "Peacock," "Jewel Band," and "Presidential" patterns in 1995. 1-3/4"d. x 4-1/2"h. $80-100 ea.

Two Pepi Herrmann bells cut in "Marc Patrick" and "Jewel" patterns in 1995. 2"d. x 4-1/4"h. $80-100 ea.

A Pepi Herrmann bell cut in 1996 in the "Marc Patrick" pattern with a golden handle. 2"d. x 4"h. $75-90.

A "one of a kind" Pepi Herrmann bell cut in 1998 in a special "Westchester" pattern and a Swarovski crystal handle. 2-3/4"d. x 6-1/2"h. $225+.

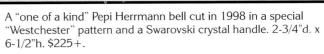

A Pepi Herrmann blue cut to clear bell in a "Wildflower" pattern designed by Hermann Defregger. 2-3/4"d x 5-1/2"h., c. 1998. $45-55.

Two Pepi Herrmann bells in "Jewel Band" and "Independence" patterns in blue cut to clear glass in 1996. Each is 1 of 5 cut. 3-1/2"d. x 7-1/2"h. $150-175 ea.

Three blue cut to clear Pepi Herrmann bells in "Marc Patrick" pattern (1 of 5), "Jewel" pattern (1 of 3), and "Romance" pattern (1 of 2). 3-1/2"d. x 7-1/2"h., 1996. $140-160 ea.

Three "one of a kind", blue cut to clear Pepi Herrmann bells. 3-1/2"d. x 7-1/2"h., 1996. $175+ ea.

This "One of a Kind" dinner bell
was designed and created at
Pepi Herrmann Crystal
of Gilford, New Hampshire
The design by Master Crystal Cutter
Pepi M. Herrmann
It is registered to
Mr. A. A. Trinidad
To be known as the "Trinidad Collection"

Pepi M. Herrmann

Pepi M. Herrmann ©1998

A Pepi Herrmann card issued for the "Trinidad Collection."

Two "one of a kind" bells designated by Pepi Herrmann in 1998 as part of the "Trinidad Collection" in red cut to clear and blue cut to clear. 3"d. x 7-1/2"h. $250+ ea.

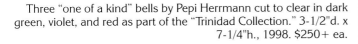

Three "one of a kind" bells by Pepi Herrmann cut to clear in amber, red, and light green as part of the "Trinidad Collection." 3-1/2"d. x 7-1/4"h., 1998. $250+ ea.

Three "one of a kind" bells by Pepi Herrmann cut to clear in dark green, violet, and red as part of the "Trinidad Collection." 3-1/2"d. x 7-1/4"h., 1998. $250+ ea.

A special "one of a kind" bell cut by Pepi Herrmann on a small "one of a kind" clear blank. This is one of the smallest cut glass bells seen by the author. 1-3/4"d. x 3"h. $150+.

Three "one of a kind" bells by Pepi Herrmann cut to clear in light green, violet, and amber as part of the "Trinidad Collection." 3-1/2"d. x 7-3/4"h., 1998. $250+ ea.

Three bells cut to clear by Pepi Herrmann in an amber "Gothic" pattern and a green "one of a kind" pattern in 1998, plus a special "one of a kind" bell in violet inscribed with the author's name and presented to him by his son's family upon becoming president of the American Bell Association in June, 1999. $250+ ea.

Three "one of a kind" bells cut to clear by Pepi Herrmann in a smaller blank in blue, amber, and green. 2"d. x 4-1/2"h., 1999. $175+ ea.

Pitkin & Brooks Company
Chicago, Illinois, 1872-1920

Pitkin & Brooks bells have a typical hexagonal handle with serrated corners and three horizontal miters. Some bells were made with slight variations of a pattern, but they were all called by the same pattern name.

Three Pitkin & Brooks Co. bells, all cut in the "Prism" pattern but with a variation in the design of the center of the eight point hobstar. Left to right: the center of the hobstar is blank, the center of the hobstar is filled with a star of eight lines, and the center of the hobstar is filled with a star of twelve lines. 3"d. x 4-1/2"h., c. 1907. $200-250 ea.

Sterling Glass Company
Cincinnati, Ohio, 1904-1950

The Sterling company produced bells in very few patterns during its existence.

L. Straus & Sons
New York, New York, 1888-1925

Straus produced many fine bells in various patterns. Most of their bells have a distinctive multifaceted top of handle.

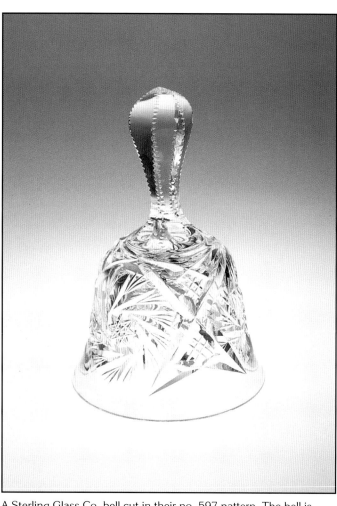

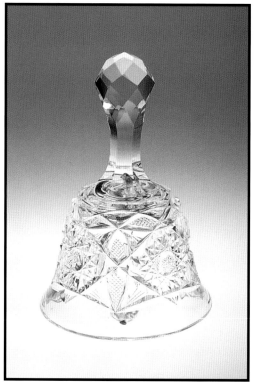

An L. Straus & Sons glass bell cut in the "Napoleon" pattern, also known as the "Perrot" pattern, patented April 16, 1895. 3"d. x 4-1/2"h. $325-375.

A Sterling Glass Co. bell cut in their no. 597 pattern. The bell is similar to Hoare's Pluto pattern. 3"d. x 4-3/4"h., c. 1917. $225-275.

A Straus glass bell cut in the "Antoinette" pattern. 3"d. x 4-1/2"h. $325-375.

A Straus bell cut in the "Corinthian" pattern. 3"d. x 4-1/2"h. $325-375.

A Straus bell in a butterfly and flower design from the "Flower Period" of cut glass. 3"d. x 4-1/2"h., c. 1920. $225-275.

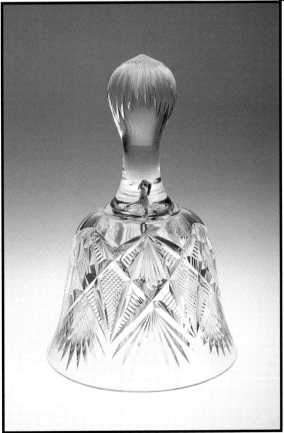

A Straus bell cut in the "Capri" pattern, patented March 14, 1893, but with a different handle cut with vertical miters. 3"d. x 4-3/4"h. $350-400.

Unger Brothers
Newark, New Jersey, 1901-1918

Unger Brothers produced bells in very few patterns. All Unger bells seen by the author have a solid silver ball clapper and chain.

An Unger Brothers bell cut in the "Rockport" pattern with a solid silver clapper and chain. 3"d. x 5"h. $250-300.

An Unger Brothers bell cut in an unknown pattern, with a solid silver clapper and chain. 3-1/4"d. x 5-1/4"h. $275-325.

An Unger Brothers bell cut in their "Standard" pattern, with a solid silver clapper and chain. 2-3/4"d. x 5-3/4"h. $275-325.

American Cut Glass Bells of Unknown Origin

The author has seen many cut glass bells which presently have not been identified. However, they are included here to illustrate the great variety of cut glass bells available to collectors — and to challenge collectors to continue researching the origin of these bells among the many firms known to have produced fine cut glass.

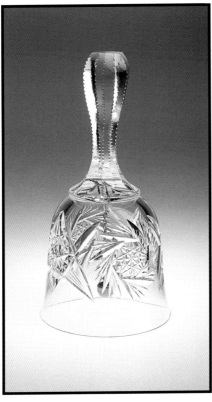

A cut glass bell with a pattern of a pinwheel alternating with an eight point star and fans in a triangle. Hexagonal handle with notched corners and flat top. 2-3/4"d. x 5-3/4"h., c. 1920s. $275-300.

A cut glass bell with a pattern of alternating stars and hobstars in diamonds on a clear blank. Unusual five-sided handle with serrated corners. 3"d. x 6"h. $300-350.

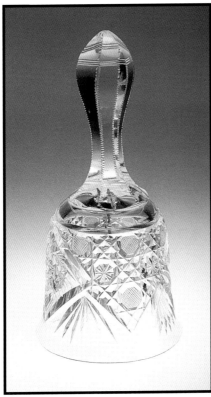

A cut glass bell with a "Harvard" and pinwheel pattern. 3"d. x 5-3/4"h. $225-275.

A cut glass bell in the same pattern as the previous bell but in a larger blank. 3-3/4"d x 7-3/4"h. $400-450.

Left: A cut glass bell in a pattern of eight point stars alternating with crosscut diamonds and punties. 3"d. x 5-3/4"h. $300-350.

Right: A cut glass bell in a pattern of hobstars alternating with crosshatched diamonds and fans. 3"d. x 5-3/4"h. $225-275.

Left: A cut glass bell in a "Russian" pattern. 3-1/4"d. x 5-3/4"h. $350-400.

Right: A cut glass bell in a pattern of two crosscut diamonds and two crosshatched diamond panels separated by fans. 3-1/2"d. x 7-1/4"h. $650-700.

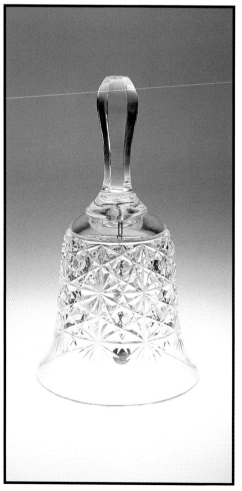

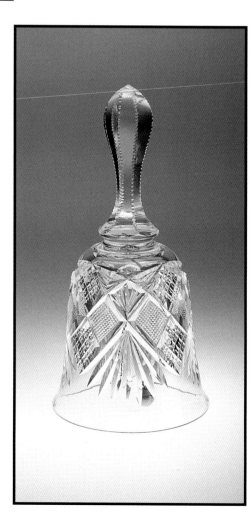

A pair of glass bells cut with six petal flowers, leaves, and a band of eight point stars. 3"d. x 4-1/2"h. $275-350 ea.

A glass bell cut with a pinwheel alternating with crosshatched diamonds and fans. 3"d. x 4-3/4"h. $225-275.

A glass bell cut in a pattern similar to the Dorflinger "Renaissance" pattern but with punties added. A star pattern is cut on the top of the handle. 3"d. x 4-1/2"h. $375-400.

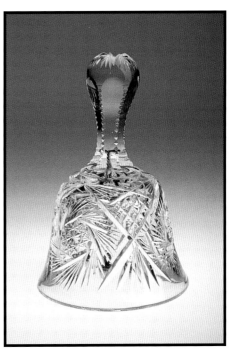

A glass bell cut in a pattern of hobstars alternating with crosscut diamonds and fans. A flashed star pattern is cut on the top of the handle. 3"d. x 4-3/4"h. $250-300.

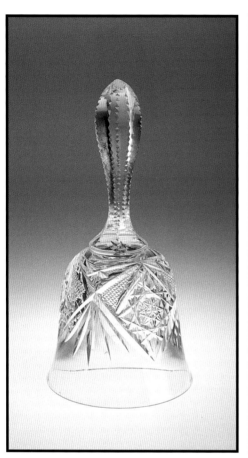

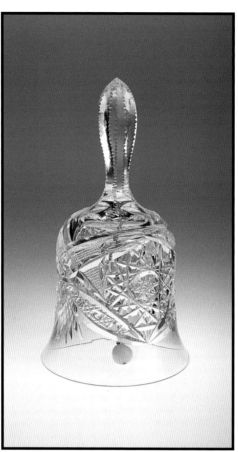

A glass bell cut with a hobstar alternating with crosscut diamonds and fan. 3"d. x 5-3/4"h. $250-300.

A glass bell cut with a sixteen point hobstar, cane, crosscut diamond, and fans. 3-1/2"d. x 6"h. $250-300.

A glass bell cut in a "Russian" pattern alternating with flowers on a stem. 3-1/4"d. x 6-1/4"h. $400-450.

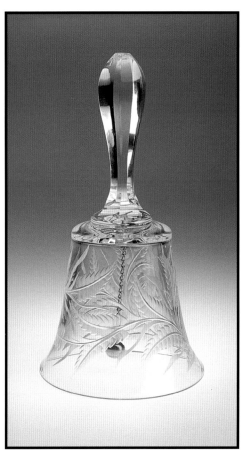 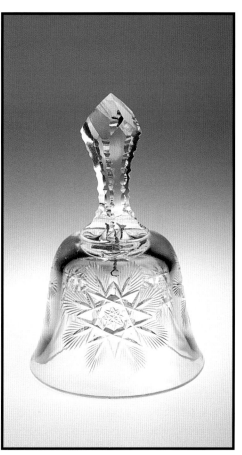 

A glass bell cut with a fern design and the initials "S. A." 3-1/2"d x 6-1/4"h. $225-275.

A bell cut in a flashed hobstar design, possibly distributed by G. W. Huntley & Co. The handle has four sides cut to a point. 3"d. x 4-3/4"h. $250-300.

A bell cut in a "Strawberry Diamond & Fan" pattern, a pattern cut by many companies. 3"d. x 5-3/4"h. $250-300.

References

Feller, John Quentin. *Dorflinger - America's Finest Glass, 1852-1921*. Marietta, Ohio: Antique Publications, 1988.

Miller, Jim. "Patriotic Motifs in Cut Glass." *Glass Collector's Digest* XIII, no. 1 (June/July 1999): 18-22.

Trinidad, A. A. Jr. "American Cut Glass Bells." *The Bell Tower* 54, no. 5 (September-October 1996): 25-36.

_____. "Ring for Service - Gently, Please." *The Hobstar* 19, no. 6 (January, 1997): 1 and 6.

_____. "Hawkes Cut Glass Bells." *Glass Collector's Digest* XII, no. 4 (December-January 1999): 70-77.

Waher, Bettye W. *The Hawkes Hunter*. Bettye W. Waher, 1984.

Chapter Four
American Engraved Glass Bells

There are many fine American glass bells that are engraved on thin glass blanks. This chapter presents some of the bells produced by some well known firms during the end of the nineteenth century and the first three-quarters of the twentieth century.

Boston & Sandwich Glass Co.
Sandwich, Massachusetts, 1870-1887

While the Boston & Sandwich Glass Co. began operations in 1826, the production of engraved bells on thin blown glass was done primarily during what is known as the Late Blown Period, 1870-1887. Bells from this period are seen engraved with names or initials surrounded by a wreath that is unique to Sandwich glass. Some bells from the company are known before this period, but it is not known if they were engraved. An invoice from the Boston & Sandwich Glass Co., dated November 22, 1861 and found in the records of the Rakow Library at the Corning Museum of Glass, lists three tea bells for 75 cents. Some cut glass bells from this company are shown in Chapter Three.

A Boston & Sandwich Glass Co. bell engraved with two pastoral scenes, garlands, and "Carrie." 3"d. x 5-1/4"h., 1870-1887. $450-500.

A close-up of one of the scenes on the Boston & Sandwich bell.

A Boston & Sandwich bell engraved with "RCB" surrounded by a wreath typical of their bells. 3"d. x 5-1/2"h., c. 1880s. $200-250.

A clear glass Boston & Sandwich bell handed down through the family of John Murray, founder of the Sandwich Cooperative Glass Co. 3-1/4"d. x 6-1/2"h. $150-200.

A Boston & Sandwich bell engraved with a "G" and a wreath. 2-1/2"d. x 4-1/4"h., c. 1880s. $200-250.

Cambridge Glass Company
Cambridge, Ohio, 1902-1958

The Cambridge Glass Company produced high quality glass items during its existence. Stemware and bells were produced from 1932 to the early 1950s in thin, plain rock crystal which was engraved or etched with a pattern. Rock crystal is a term originally given to objects carved from natural crystals; by the 1920s the term was used to describe thin glass engraved and given a polished finish.

The company did not issue catalogs on an annual basis, but produced them occasionally and then supplemented the catalog by issuing circular letters which included pages that could be inserted to update the catalog. Examples of the patterns used for their bells can be seen on a Cambridge catalog page issued around the 1940s. The most popular bell patterns were Rose Point and Chantilly. Any Cambridge bells are highly collectible.

Cambridge bell handles have very distinctive pressed patterns. Clappers consist of a round bead with a thin chain embedded in the glass via a drilled hole filled with a cement or plaster.

Two Cambridge Glass Co. bells in clear etched glass. The bell on the left has a "Blossom Time" pattern on a #3700 stem handle and is 2-1/4"d. x 5-1/4"h. The bell on the right has a "Chantilly" pattern on a #3625 stem handle and is 3-3/4"d. x 6-1/4"h. $80-100 ea.

Two Cambridge Glass Co. bells with a #3575 stem lyre handle. The bell on the left is clear and is 2-1/2"d. x 5-3/4"h. $30-40. The bell on the right has a "Diane" etched pattern and is 2-1/2"d. x 5-3/4"h. $90-100.

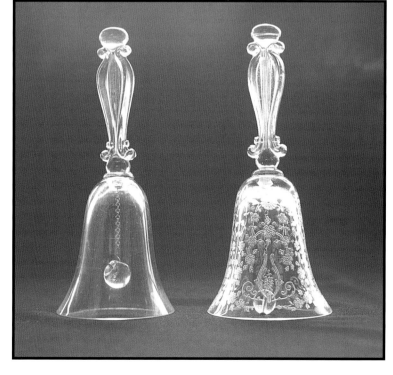

Two Cambridge Glass Co. bells with #3130 stem handles. The bell on the left has an engraved "Manor" pattern; the bell on the right has an etched "Portia" pattern. 2-1/2"d. x 6-1/4"h. $60-70 ea.

Two Cambridge Glass Co. bells with #3650 stem handles. The bell on the left has an etched "Wildflower" design; the bell on the right has an engraved "Montrose" design. 2-3/4"d. x 5"h. $40-50 ea.

A label used on Cambridge Glass Co. bells.

T. G. Hawkes & Company
Corning, New York, 1880-1962

Cut glass bells produced by the Hawkes company primarily during the Brilliant Period of American cut glass are presented in Chapter Three. This chapter presents the company's later bells cut and engraved on thin lead glass.

From about 1913 to 1917, Hawkes produced a series of copper wheel engraved bells, using some very elaborate advertisements for them. Starting in the 1920s, Hawkes produced many bells with sterling silver tops of handle. The author is aware of at least twelve patterns produced on six different stems with sterling tops over a forty year period. As noted in Chapter Three, Hawkes sometimes salvaged broken stems by converting them to bells. During and after the 1920s, the company salvaged some broken stemware by making them into bells with sterling silver tops.

In the 1950s, Hawkes made some engraved glass bells mounted in silver frames. The patterns of some of the bells in these frames are the same as those produced with silver handles.

A T. G. Hawkes & Co. glass bell engraved with the "Kismet" pattern, signed HAWKES on shoulder. 3-1/4"d. x 5-1/2"h., c. 1913. $100-125.

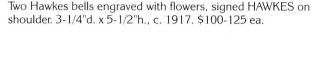

Two Hawkes bells engraved with flowers, signed HAWKES on shoulder. 3-1/4"d. x 5-1/2"h., c. 1917. $100-125 ea.

Two Hawkes bells with sterling silver handles, likely made from broken stemware. Left: engraved "Pearl Border," 3-3/4"d. x 4-3/4"h., $50. Right: engraved "Sheraton Border," 3"d. x 6"h., $60.

Two Hawkes bells with sterling silver handles, c. 1940s. Left to right: engraved "Chantilly," 2-3/4"d. x 5-3/4"h.; engraved "Avalon," 2-3/4"d. x 5-1/2"h. $70-90 ea.

Two Hawkes bells with sterling silver handles, c. 1940s. Left to right: engraved "Sheraton Border," 2-3/4"d. x 5-1/2"h.; engraved "Pearl Border," 2-3/4"d. x 5-3/4"h. $70-90 ea.

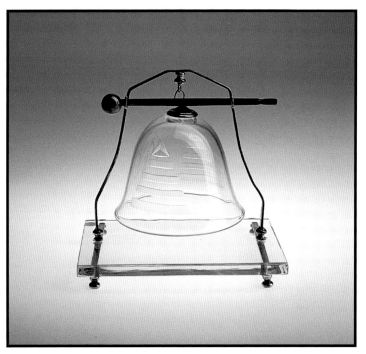

A Hawkes bell engraved in a tree design and supported on a sterling silver frame with glass base and a separate striking hammer. 2-3/4"h. (overall height 4-1/4"), c. 1950s. $175-225.

A Hawkes bell engraved in the "Puritan" pattern supported on a 6-3/4"h. sterling silver frame with a glass base and a separate striking hammer. 2-3/4"d. x 4"h., c. 1950s. $225-275.

A. H. Heisey & Company
Newark, Ohio, 1896-1957

Heisey produced many fine glass bells of high quality lead crystal with engraved and etched patterns. All were made from blown, clear thin blanks and pressed glass handles. The original clappers are of multifaceted glass on a thin chain inserted into a drilled hole filled with plaster.

Heisey glass bells, as well as their other stemware, are identified by a name and a number of the etching or engraving on the body of the bell, as well as a name and number for the pattern on the handle. Numbers associated with the more common Heisey bells are as follows:

Bell Handle:		Etched Design:		Engraved Design:	
Jamestown	3408	Rosalie	497	Daisy	924
Kimberly	4091	Minuet	503	Barcelona	941
Graceful	5022	Orchid	507	Narcissus	965
Tyrolean	5025	Heisey Rose	515	Sheffield	985
Rose	5072				

Heisey also produced pressed molded Victorian Belle glass bells in colorless clear and frosted glass (see Chapter Five). The well known Heisey trademark of an H in a diamond was never marked on blown wares, only on pressed items. Sometimes this mark can be found on the pressed handle of the blown and etched bells and also on the pressed Victorian Belle.

After the close of the Heisey company, many molds and design patents were sold in 1958 to the Imperial Glass Company of Bellaire, Ohio. Few of the hundreds of designs produced by Heisey were made into bells. Any Heisey etched or engraved bell is a fine addition to a bell collection.

Two A. H. Heisey & Co. bells in an etched #507 "Orchid" pattern. The bell on the left is on a #5022 Graceful stem, 2-1/4"d. x 5-1/4"h. The bell on the right is on a #5025 Tyrolean stem, 2-3/4"d. x 5-1/4"h. 1940-1957. $90-110 ea.

Two A. H. Heisey & Co. engraved bells on #3408 Jamestown stems. The bell on the left has a #924 "Daisy" pattern; the bell on the right has a #941 "Barcelona" pattern with an "H" in a diamond Heisey molded mark on the center of the molded handle. 2-3/4"d. x 4-3/4"h., c. 1940. $80-90 ea.

A Heisey etched #503 "Minuet" pattern bell on a #3408 Jamestown stem. One of the most popular of Heisey's etchings. 2-3/4"d. x 4-3/4"h., 1939-1950. $80-90.

A Heisey bell in an engraved "Moonglo" pattern. 3-1/2"d. x 6-1/2"h. $90 -100.

A Heisey etched #515 "Heisey Rose" pattern bell on a #5072 Rose stem. 3"d. x 5-1/2"h., 1949-1953. $110-125.

A Heisey bell in a blown "Diamond Optic" design with a green molded handle. 2-1/2"d. x 4-1/4"h. $100-110.

Seneca Glass Company
Morgantown, West Virginia, 1891-1983

Seneca made many fine bells on very thin, blown lead glass in the 1960s and 1970s. The bells, with a few exceptions, have the unique feature of a hollow handle through which the chain, holding a crystal clapper, passes to the top of the handle and is held there by a metal pinhead, flat spiral, or star. The bells were made in several heights, but primarily in heights of 3 3/4", 4 1/2", and 5 1/2". A small 2 1/4" hanging Christmas bell with a gold rim, but without a handle, was produced in 1978 and 1979. Seneca decorated its glass by acid etching, needle etching, plate etching, and engraving. In the 1970s, Seneca produced some bells in colored glass but these generally were not decorated.

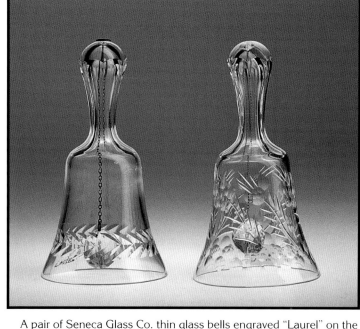

A pair of Seneca Glass Co. thin glass bells engraved "Laurel" on the left and "cut 771" on the right. The chain passing through the hollow handle is supported at the top by a spiral coil on the "Laurel" bell and the more usual pinhead type terminal on the "cut 771" bell. 2"d. x 2-3/4"h. $30-50 ea.

The spiral coil at the top of the "Laurel" Seneca bell.

Six point star at top of the bell with wedding rings clapper.

Three Seneca Glass Co. bells. Left to right: a clear bell with entwined wedding bells and dove clapper, engraved with map of West Virginia for 1963 centennial, engraved for 1976 Bicentennial. 2-1/2"d. x 4-1/2"h. $40-60 ea.

Three Seneca Glass bells, engraved (left to right) in the "Orleans," "Stratford," and "Swirled Optic" patterns. 2-1/2"d. x 4-1/2"h. $30-40 ea.

Three Seneca bells, left to right: "Puritan" pattern, engraved "Laurel," and "Cut 796" with unpolished vertical miters. 2-1/2"d. x 4-1/2"h. $25-35 ea.

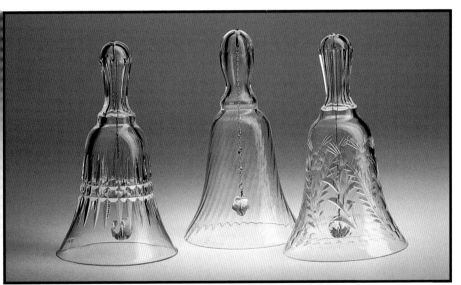

Three Seneca bells, left to right: "Cut 859," "Swirled Optic Fascination," "Margery Cut 771" with a seven sided handle and a white ball holding chain at top. 3"d. x 5-1/2"h. $40-50 ea.

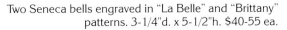

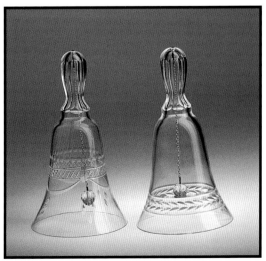

Two Seneca bells engraved in "La Belle" and "Brittany" patterns. 3-1/4"d. x 5-1/2"h. $40-55 ea.

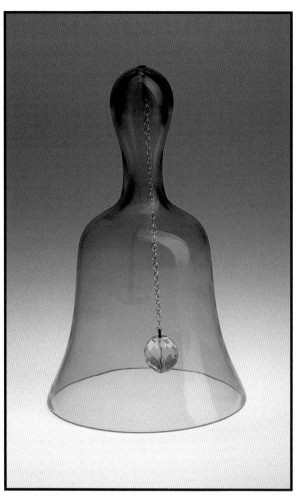

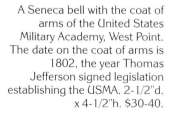

Clear blue and clear green Seneca bells. 3"d. x 5-1/2"h. $50-65 ea.

A clear blue Seneca bell. 2-1/2"d. x 4-1/2"h. $50-60.

A Seneca bell with the coat of arms of the United States Military Academy, West Point. The date on the coat of arms is 1802, the year Thomas Jefferson signed legislation establishing the USMA. 2-1/2"d. x 4-1/2"h. $30-40.

A Seneca Christmas bell ornament with a gold rim, dated 1978. 2"d. x 2-1/4"h. $15-25.

American Engraved Glass Bells of Unknown Origin

There were many glass companies producing engraved glass bells from the 1920s, but some have not been identified with a specific company as of this writing. Presented herein are some of the bells that fall into the unknown category.

A clear glass bell with engraved garlands and a ring handle, signed with "D". 2"d. x 2-1/4"h., c. 1982. $25-30.

A thistle shaped bell engraved with stars alternating with punties, and a ring pattern handle. 2-1/2"d. x 5-1/2"h. $30-40.

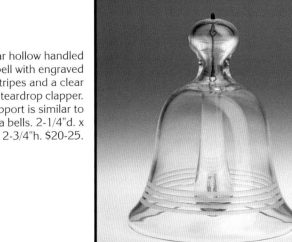

A clear hollow handled bell with engraved stripes and a clear teardrop clapper. Support is similar to Seneca bells. 2-1/4"d. x 2-3/4"h. $20-25.

References

Barlow, Raymond E., and Joan E. Kaiser. *The Glass Industry of Sandwich, Volume 4.* Windham, New Hampshire: L Barlow-Kaiser Publishing Co., Inc., 1983.

Cambridge Glass Company. *Fine Handmade Table Glassware,* 1940 catalog reprint. National Cambridge Collectors, Inc., 1995: page 444.

Lindbeck, Jennifer A. and Jeffrey B. Snyder. *Elegant Seneca.* Atglen, Pennsylvania: Schiffer Publishing, Ltd., 2000.

Page, Bob and Dale Fredericksen. *Seneca Glass Co. 1891-1983.* Greensboro, North Carolina: Page-Fredericksen Publishing Co., 1995.

Trinidad, A. A. Jr. "Cambridge Glass Bells." *The Bell Tower* 53, no. 3 (May-June 1995): 24, 25.

_____. "Central Glass Works Bells" *The Bell Tower* 57, no. 52 (March-April 1999): 33.

_____. "Late Depression Quality Glass Heisey Bells." *The Bell Tower* 50, no. 5 (September-October 1992): 17, 18.

_____. "Sandwich Glass Crystal Bells." *The Bell Tower* 53, no. 5 (September-October 1995): 10, 11.

Willey, Harold E. *Heisey's Cut Handmade Glassware.,* Newark, Ohio: 1974

Chapter Five
American Blown and Pressed Glass Bells

American blown and pressed glass bells are known from the middle of the nineteenth century. Many of the earlier bells in pressed glass patterns were produced in imitation of the more expensive cut glass patterns produced before and after the beginning of the twentieth century.

Many of the American companies who have produced blown and pressed glass bells are presented here in alphabetical order. Note that few of the companies have survived to the present time.

Abelman Art Glass
Anaheim, California

Stuart Abelman has been well known in art glass circles for his many forms of art glass in rich detail. In 1979, he made a bell in iridescent colors, limited to 1,500 and signed and dated by Abelman.

A Stuart Abelman art glass bell in iridescent colors, #222/1,500. Dated 1979 on the top of the handle and signed Abelman along the inside of rim. 3-1/2"d. x 7"h. $100-125.

Akro Agate Company
Clarksburg, West Virginia, 1911-1951

The Akro Agate Company started its operations producing colorful marbles. Because of competition with other marble manufacturers, the company started to produce novelty items, including bells, in the 1930s. Initially, the bells were made as cosmetic containers for Lander Distributors of New York. They can be found as covers for round, closely fitted red-rimmed cardboard containers holding one to three perfume bottles. Sometimes a red tassel is tied to the bell.

The bells have either a smocking or ribbed pattern. The smocking pattern bells can be found in yellow, orange, white, ivory, and various shades of green and blue, as well as in clear glass. A rare color is transparent pink. The ribbed pattern is found in clear glass and a rare transparent green.

An iron clapper is supported on a wire that is attached to two glass prongs. On the inside near the prongs can be found the Akro Agate mark, a flying crow holding two marbles (agates), together with "Made in USA."

When Akro Agate closed in 1951, the bell molds were sold to the Guernsey Glass Company of Cambridge, Ohio. The owner of that company, Harold Bennett, substituted a "B" for the Akro mark on the bells. The original Akro molds had a six sided handle whose sides carried down to the shoulder of the bell. On the bells reproduced by Guernsey Glass, the base of the handle is rounded instead of having the six sides continue before meeting the shoulder.

Three Akro Agate Co. "Smocking" pattern bells in pumpkin, clear pink, and green. The Akro Agate mark (of a flying crow holding agates) and Made in USA are molded on either side of the two glass prongs holding the stiff wire and iron clapper, typical of all Akro Agate bells. 3-1/4"d. x 5-1/2"h., c. 1930s. Left to right: $140-180; $400-450; $100-150. This bell can also be found in yellow, $400-450.

Three Akro Agate Co. "Smocking" pattern bells in various shades of blue, one with a streak of green. 3-1/4"d. x 5-1/2"h. $70-90 ea.

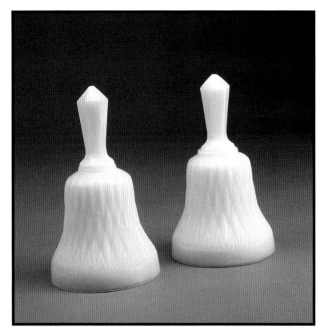

Two Akro Agate "Smocking" pattern bells, custard colored and white. 3-1/4"d. x 5-1/2"h. $40-50 ea.

Clear glass Akro Agate bells in a "Smocking" pattern used as tops for perfume bottle cardboard container gift sets holding one to three bottles of Lander perfumes. Bottom of red rimmed cardboard is sometimes labeled Lander Distributors or Wheatley, Fifth Ave., New York with the name of the perfume. Some bells are found with a red tassel. $25-50 ea.

Clear glass Akro Agate bells. Left to right: "Smocking" pattern, 3-1/2"d. x 5-1/2"h., $20-25; "Smocking" pattern, 1-3/4"d. x 3"h., $30-40; "Ribbed" pattern, 3-1/4"d. x 5-1/2"h., $20-25. The "Ribbed" pattern can also be found in clear green, $400-450.

Boston & Sandwich Glass Company
Sandwich, Massachusetts, 1870-1887

Engraved glass bells by the Boston & Sandwich Glass Company are presented in Chapter Four. During that same period, the company produced bells in opal glass painted with herons, flowers, and leaves. Some of this decoration has been attributed to the Smith Brothers of New Bedford, Massachusetts.

A Boyd's Crystal Art Glass Co. "Woodsie the Owl" bell in cobalt blue with a "B" in a diamond mark. 2-1/4"d. x 3-1/2"h., c. 1978-1983. $20-25.

A Boston & Sandwich Glass Co. bell in opal glass painted with a pink overlay and autumn leaves. 3"d. x 5-1/2"h., c. 1880s. $200-225.

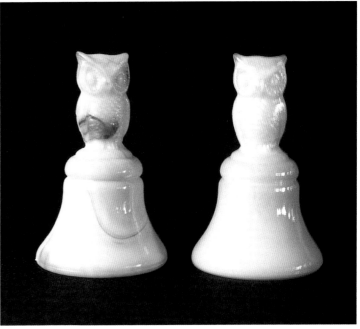

Two Boyd's Crystal Art Glass Co. "Woodsie the Owl" bells in blue/white slag and pearl white. Molded with a "B" in a diamond with one bar. 2-1/4"d. x 3-1/2"h., c. 1983-1988. $20-25 ea.

Boyd's Crystal Art Glass, Inc.
Cambridge, Ohio, 1978-

Boyd's Crystal Art Glass company has made several glass bells, some from molds acquired from glass companies that have gone out of business. A popular bell is "Woodsie the Owl," which was made in twenty different colors from 1984 to 1986. Thereafter, the bell in new colors has been made once each year. Boyd's "Louise" figurine bell became an annual series starting in 1979.

The company trademark is a B in a diamond. Starting in 1978, the company has added a line to the diamond every five years, so that by 1998 the diamond was enclosed in a rectangle.

A Boyd's Crystal Art Glass "Louise" figurine bell in a brown slag glass. Molded with a "B" in a diamond enclosed by four bars and with a "5". This bell can be found in many colors. 2-3/4"d. x 4-1/4"h., c. 1998. $20-25.

Bryce Brothers Company
Mt. Pleasant, Pennsylvania, 1895-1965

Bryce Brothers has a long company history starting in 1850 as Bryce, McKee and Company. There are some colorful bells that have been attributed to various glass companies, but the author believes they were made by Bryce Brothers. A Bryce Brothers catalog of 1942-1950 shows stemware, in pattern 894 and design patent 120136, with stems matching the handles of bells shown here. Clear glass bells having the same shape may have been engraved by the Lotus Glass Co., who made no glass but are known to have bought blanks from Bryce Brothers.

Three Bryce Brothers Co. bells. The engraved diamond design on the clear bell may have been engraved by the Lotus Glass Co. 3"d. x 5-1/4"h., c. 1940s. $30-40 ea.

Central Glass Company
Wheeling, West Virginia, 1867-1939

During its early years, the Central Glass Co. produced clear, pressed tableware in many patterns. Around 1896, the company became famous for the production of coin glass. All kinds of glass articles were made with impressions of silver dollars, half dollars, quarters, and dimes. In the early part of the twentieth century, Central produced clear thin crystal stemware in many colors. During this period, the company also made clear, colored, crystal bells. These bells typically have a swirled tapered handle with a hexagonal base. The colored glass is in the body of the bell or in the handle. Some bells have geometric

or floral patterns engraved. A few bells are found accompanied by a matching under-plate.

Central bells are also known in clear glass and etched, or otherwise marked to commemorate special events. A few are known with a sterling silver overlay. All of the bells have a wire embedded in the glass to hold a chain and a two part hollow metal clapper typical of American bells from that era.

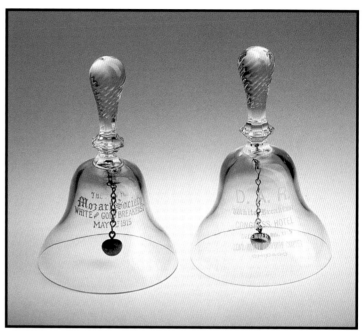

Two Central Glass Co. bells made to commemorate special gatherings. On the left, a bell decorated in gold with "New York Mozart Society, White and Gold Breakfast, May 1, 1915." On the right, a bell etched with "D.A.R. White Breakfast, Congress Hotel, December 8th, 1915, Gen'l Henry Dearborn Chapter, Chicago." 3-1/4"d. x 5"h. $90-110 ea.

In 1919, Central acquired molds for thicker glass bells with a raised rim from the Jefferson Glass Company. These bells are found in clear glass with engraved decoration and etched to commemorate events and places. A clear glass bell with the

A clear glass bell in the Oglebay Institute Mansion Museum, Wheeling, West Virginia, with a Central Glass Co. label. 3"d. x 6-1/4"h., c. 1925. *Courtesy of the Collection of the Museums of Oglebay Institute, Wheeling, WV.*

Five Central Glass Co. bells in various colors, two engraved, and one with silver overlay. 3-1/4"d. x 4-3/4"h., c. 1915. Colored glass $50-100. Silver overlay $150-175.

original Central Glass Company label is displayed at the Oglebay Institute Glass Museum in Wheeling, West Virginia. Some of the clear glass bells were cut with floral patterns.

Three Central Glass Co. bells with raised rims. Molds obtained from the Jefferson Glass Co. in 1919. Left to right: engraved leaves and etched Clarksburg, W. V. 1929; clear glass; engraved floral design. 3"d. x 6-1/4"h., c. 1920s. $40-60 ea.

Crystal Art Glass Company
Cambridge, Ohio, 1947-1978

The Crystal Art Glass Company was started by John and Elizabeth Degenhart to produce paperweights, but around 1965 the company started reproducing glass articles. Any bells (which have no clappers) produced by the company after 1972 are embossed with a D in a heart. In 1978, the company was sold to Bernard Boyd who formed Boyd's Crystal Art Glass, Inc.

Three Crystal Art Glass Co. bells molded for the Bicentennial. They have a D in a heart, for Degenhart, on the inside top of bell and 1776-1976 on the outside. 2-1/4"d. x 2-1/4"h. $20-25 ea.

Dalzell-Viking Glass Company
New Martinsville, West Virginia,
1987-1998

In 1986, the past president of the Fostoria Glass Company, Kenneth Dalzell, bought the Viking Glass Company to form the Dalzell-Viking Glass Company. Bells were produced starting in 1989, primarily from molds acquired from other companies. The company produced some of the Victorian Belle bells for the Heisey Collectors of America using the Heisey molds in the possession of that collectors' organization.

Fenton Art Glass Company
Williamstown, West Virginia, 1905-

The Fenton Art Glass Company is the oldest American glass company still in continuous operation. The company produced its first pressed glass bell in carnival glass in 1911 as a souvenir for the Elks convention in Atlantic City, New Jersey. A 1910 trade journal noted that the Woolworth five and ten cent store had ordered 320 dozen bells showing an Elks head. A bell made for the 1917 Elks convention in Portland, Oregon was sold at auction for $22,500 at a 1990s American Carnival Glass Association convention. All these bells have a handle with concentric rings and a heavy chain and clapper.

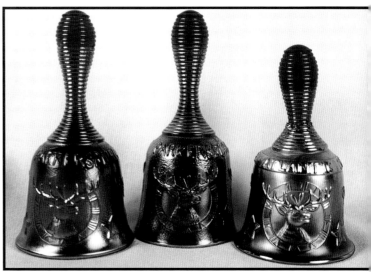

Two Fenton 1914 Parkersburg carnival glass bells on the left and a 1911 Atlantic City carnival glass bell on the right, made for Elks Club conventions. The Atlantic City bell on the right was damaged and has been repaired. The BPOE met in Atlantic City from July 10 through July 13, 1911; Mr. Frank M. Fenton reports that this event was called a "Grand Reunion." Fenton records show that they shipped 5,000 pieces to the F. W. Woolworth Co., who in turn sold them at the convention. 6"d x 2-3/4"h. $2,500+ ea. *Courtesy of Frank M. Fenton, The Fenton Glass Museum.*

One of the oldest Fenton bells, first produced around 1913, is the Daisy Cut bell, a design with a star in a diamond covering the body of the bell and having a four sided tapered handle with serrated corners. The bell has a very heavy chain and clapper, and first appeared in a 1914 Fenton catalog as a tea bell. The original production illustrated in catalogs shows a marigold carnival glass bell and a clear glass bell. However, cobalt blue and ruby colored bells having the same heavy chain exist and were probably made during the same period. Using the same mold, Fenton produced this bell again from about 1933 to 1936. These later bells in clear, ruby, and cobalt blue have a stiff wire and lead clapper. The ruby bells sometimes have an amber handle. Some of the clear bells were issued with souvenir markings superimposed. All the Daisy Cut bells have the words PATD APPLD molded around the glass prongs where the chain or wire is attached.

Fenton Art Glass Co. #47 tea bell, "Daisy Cut" pattern in royal blue, marigold carnival (known earlier as Golden Iridescent), clear, and ruby, with heavy chain and sinker type clapper. Four-sided tapered handles with serrated corners. PATD APPLD is molded around glass prongs holding the chain. 3"d. x 5-3/4"h., 1908-1928. Marigold bell $350-375. Others $50-60.

Fenton Art Glass Co. bells in the "Daisy Cut" pattern in ruby, clear, and royal blue with wire and lead clapper. PATD APPLD is molded around glass prongs holding the chain. 3"d. x 5-3/4"h., 1933-1939. $40-50 ea.

In 1967, Fenton started producing Hobnail bells in colonial colors and milk glass. In 1970, they began producing a carnival glass Daisy and Button (D&B) bell as part of their Olde Virginia line of glass. In 1971, the D&B design became part of the regular line and the bell was produced in many colors as pattern 1966 with plain rim and pattern 1967 with ruffled rim. Some have been issued as souvenir items. The handles of D&B bells have concentric rings similar to the Elks bells.

Some books on Fenton glass state that the first D&B bells were produced in 1970 and no bells were made between 1937 and 1967. However, the author has a clear D&B bell with a heavy chain and clapper similar to that used in the Elks bells and 1913 Daisy Cut bells. In correspondence with the author, Mr. Frank M. Fenton stated that he believes the pattern on the molds for the Elks bells was removed and replaced with the D&B pattern. In searching Fenton's 1937 records, Mr. Fenton found a #1900 D&B bell listed in clear crystal with a yearend inventory of thirty dozen clear D&B bells in stock. Number 1900 was a number assigned to various D&B items in 1937 and 1938. Mr. Fenton also stated that this was still the Depression era and Fenton was trying to save money. Apparently, the old clappers used originally with the Elks and early Daisy Cut bells were still available and used on the 1937 D&B bells. The D&B mold used in 1937 was then resurrected and used again in 1970.

Five Fenton bells in "Daisy & Button" pattern, mold #1966, in frosted mint, purple carnival, marigold carnival, frosted blue, and cream, with wire and lead or iron clapper. 3-1/2"d. x 5-3/4"h., 1970s and 1980s. $25-35 ea.

Fenton bells in "Daisy & Button" pattern, mold #1967, with flared ruffled rim, in blue Burmese, amber, chocolate, red, blue, green, and yellow, with chain and crystal clapper. 3-3/4"d. x 5-3/4"h., 1980s and 1990s. Blue Burmese and chocolate bells $60-80. Others $25-35.

A Fenton bell in the clear "Daisy & Button" pattern, originally the #1900 pattern, with a heavy chain and clapper. 3-1/2"d. x 5-3/4"h., c. 1937. $60-70.

Most Fenton bells have an applied paper label. However, starting in 1970 for carnival glass items and in 1972 for other items, the company impressed the name "Fenton" into an oval in the glass. Starting in 1980, an "8" was added and this number changed with each decade. In 1983, the company impressed a script "f" in an oval for glass produced from molds acquired from other companies. In 1984, a script "f" overlapping a circle started to be used on sand blasted articles and on paper labels. Bells made for the television shopping channel QVC have a "C" prefix on the pattern number.

Since 1970 Fenton has used hundreds of different patterns and designs for pressed glass and blown glass bells, so that presently they are the most prolific producer of glass bells in the United States.

Fenton bells in the "Currier and Ives Old Mill" pattern in blue over white and rust over white. 3-1/2"d. x 7"h., 1980s. $25-35 ea.

Two Fenton bells in the "Lily of the Valley" pattern in blue Burmese and blue.
3-1/2"d. x 5-1/2"h., 1970s. $20-40 ea.

Fenton bells in the "Madonna" pattern, mold # 9467, in purple carnival, blue, white, Independence Blue iridescent, and ruby iridescent. 3-1/2"d. x 6-1/2"h., 1970s. $20-30 ea.

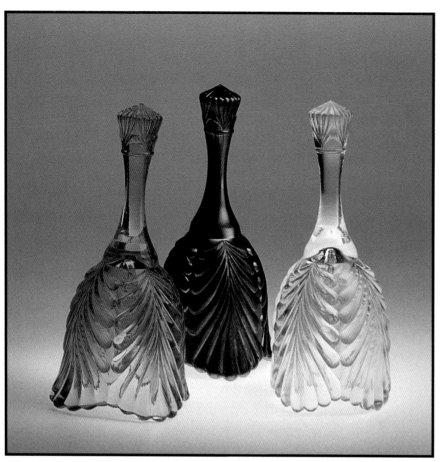

Fenton bells in mold #9665, in clear cranberry, blue-green carnival, and clear. 3"sq. x 6-1/2"h., 1980s. $20-30 ea.

A Fenton bell in the "Sable Arch" pattern, mold #9065, in amethyst carnival, made from Red-Cliff Co. molds. 3-3/4"d. x 5-3/4"h., 1990s. $30-40.

Two Fenton bells in mold #7564, in tan with painted violets and Bristol Blue PK. 3-1/2"d. x 6"h., 1980s. $25-30 ea.

A Fenton bell in the "Temple" pattern with a butterfly finial in red carnival, 3-1/2"d. x 6-1/2"h., 1990s. $30-40.

A ruby red Fenton bell with painted rose, mold #9660. 4"d. x 7"h., 1970s. $30-40.

Two Fenton bells in mold #8465 in blue BU, and amber AR, 4"d. x 5"h., c. 1977, plus a spruce green #CV085SI bell from the museum collection, 4-1/4"d. x 5-1/2"h., c. 1995. $30-40 ea.

Fenton bells in "Faberge" pattern, mold #8466, in purple carnival CN, lavender LN, rose pearl iridescent DN, frosted crystal velvet VE, carnival pink, cranberry DK, and rosalene RE. 3-1/2"d. x 6-1/2"h., 1970s through 1990s. $25-50 ea.

Two Fenton bells in "Faberge" pattern, 1980s: mold #9466VO in pink with white scalloped rim, 3"d. x 6-3/4"h.; mold #8264NK in purple carnival, 3-3/4"d. x 6-3/4"h. $30-40 ea.

Three Fenton bells (left to right): pink opalescent, with scalloped rim and painted flowers, from QVC #C5380. 4-3/4"d. x 6-1/4"h., 1993. $40-50; special rosalene, with reversed pineapple design. 3"d. x 6-1/2"h., 1994. $60-70; country cranberry with clear handle, mold #6590CC. 3-1/2"d x 6-1/4"h., 1993. $60-70.

Left: Fenton bell in aqua carnival, mold #8362OI, with an open ruffled lattice skirt. 4"d. x 6-3/4"h., c. 1989. Right: Fenton bell in green iridescent, mold 39560GZ. 3-3/4"d. x 6-1/2"h., c. 1990. $40-50 ea.

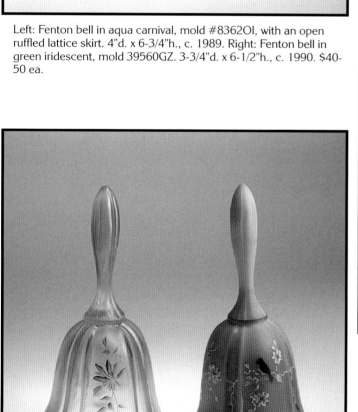

Fenton paisley design bells in (left to right): white with painted violets, clear violet rim, mold #2746PJ. 4-1/2"d. x 7"h., c. 1995. $40-50; white with painted flowers, mold #6761ES. 4"d. x 6-3/4"h., c. 1989. $30-40; ruby with amberina handle, mold #6760RU. 3-1/2"d. x 6-3/4"h., c. 1991. $25-35.

Left: Fenton bell in gold pearl "Aurora" pattern, mold #9667GF, with a painted flower. 3-3/4"d. x 6-3/4"h., c. 1990. $45-60. Right: Fenton bell in rosalene satin, mold #9667KT, with painted bluebird from the 1989 Connoisseur Collection. 3-1/2"d. x 7"h. $85-100.

Three Fenton musical Christmas bells in mold #7669. Left to right: ND color with painted candle, 1994; DZ color with painted flowers and barn, 1993; ZX color in mother-of-pearl painted with flowers, 1992. 3-1/2"d. x 6-1/4"h. $50-70 ea.

One of five Fenton Campbell Kids bells, mold #7668K2, opaque lemon painted with "Summer Fun." 3-1/4"d. x 6-1/4"h., c. 1985. $40-50.

Two Fenton bells in custard glass, mold #8267, with painted black-eyed Susans and daisies. 3-1/2"d. x 6-3/4"h., c. 1990s. $30-40 ea.

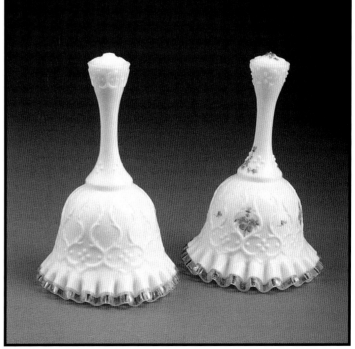

Two Fenton bells in "Spanish Lace" pattern, mold #3567, with clear ruffled rims. One in milk glass, SC, and one with painted flowers, DV. 4-1/4"d. x 6-1/4"h., 1970s. $30-40 ea.

Two Fenton bells in mold #9465, an inverted strawberry pattern, in clear lavender and blue Burmese. 3-1/2"d. x 6"h., c. 1980s. $30-50 ea.

Three Fenton bells in similar molds: a black bell with painted copper rose in a #7666KP mold made for QVC in 1990. 4-1/4"d. x 7"h.; a velva rose bell in 7562VR mold made for Fenton's 75th anniversary in 1980. "75th" is molded near the prongs holding the chain and clapper. 4-1/4"d. x 7-1/2"h.; and a white bell with caramel edge in mold #5039. 4-3/4"d. x 7"h., c. 1990s. $50-70 ea.

Three Fenton Burmese glass bells in mold #7562: a satin finish on a 1983 bell with painted flower, 847/2000; a plain satin finish bell, c. 1984; and a plain glazed finish bell, c. 1984. 4-1/2"d. x 7"h. $60-80 ea.

Fenton satin finish Burmese glass bells. Left to right: mold #7666SB, painted shells motif, 4"d. x 6-1/4"h., 1986, 494/2500; painted flower, 2-1/4"d. x 4-1/2"h., 1985, 551/3500; mold #7666EB, 4"d. x 6"h., 1985, 1691/2500; mold #7662WQ, made for Mary Walrath, 2-1/4"d. x 4-1/4"h., 1986; mold #7666, 3-3/4"d. x 6-1/4"h., c. 1990. Large bells $100-120 ea. Small bells $50-60 ea.

Fenton Patriots, or Bicentennial bells, portraying Washington, Jefferson, Lafayette, and Franklin in Independence Blue carnival, mold #8467IB; Valley Forge white, mold #8467VW; Patriot Red, mold #8467PR, and Chocolate, mold #8467CK. 3-1/2"d. x 6-1/2"h., 1976. $30-40 ea.

A Fenton satin finish Rose Burmese bell made for QVC, Whitton mold #9066RB, Museum Collection. 4-1/2"d. x 6-1/4"h., 1997. $70 -90.

Three other variations of the Fenton Patriots bells: dark Patriot Red, mold #8467PR; satin white, mold #8467WS; and clear carnival. 3-1/2"d. x 6-1/2"h. $40-50 ea.

Fischer Crystal Bells
Overland Park, Kansas, 1972–

Fischer Crystal Bells is a division of Creative Merchandising, Inc. Soon after it started, it was one of the largest producers of crystal bells in the United States. By the early 1980s, it was producing over sixty thousand bells a year, both for company use and for others, including Goebel's Hummelwerk Division, Germany. The company has operated under the control of Glen Jones, who has guided the design and production using special equipment.

Many of the bells produced over the years started as crystal goblets imported from France, Germany, and other countries. The base was removed, the cut edge was smoothed, the bell was decorated or etched, and a clapper was added. Similar bells today are produced and sold with a variety of figural and other ceramic clappers. However, bells popular with bell collectors have been decorated with a design produced by a method called "deep abrasive etching," developed by the Jones company in 1975 using semi-automated machines to do the cutting by an air blast containing grit. The design to be cut on the bell was developed as a mask and placed on the bell blank; then a thin layer of the exposed glass surrounding the mask was removed using the special machine.

The first bells produced by this method in 1975 used a clear glass blank. A limited edition of 5,000 bells was made for a Mother's Day bell, followed by a limited edition of 5,000 Christmas bells. Using the same method, the company produced a unique 1978-1980 series of Christmas bells in colored cased glass. The colored cased blanks were made by Tritschler Winterhalder in Germany, no longer operating. Some of these bells were signed by Glen Jones on the handle and were given a serial number of 10,000 on the clear handle. The first bell in the series, from 1978, was in cased ruby red. It was followed by a cobalt blue in 1979 and an emerald green in 1980. The red bell was issued by Goebel and their mark is lo-

cated on the top of the clear handle. As Goebel did not actually manufacture them, the 1979 and 1980 bells do not have the Goebel mark and were issued under the name of Hummelwerk.

Glen Jones has since used some of the cased colored blanks to produce limited editions with various patterns.

Cased Colored Glass Bells by Glen Jones

Year	Pattern	Issued by	Color Made	No.
1978	The Choir	Goebel	Ruby Red	10,000
1978	Maple Leaf	Goebel	Ruby Red	100
1979	Nativity	Hummelwerk	Cobalt Blue	10,000
1980	Star of David	Glen Jones	Cobalt Blue	*100
1980	Three Wise Men	Hummelwerk	Emerald Green	*7,000
1980	Doves	Glen Jones	Emerald Green	*200
1980	Clipper Ship	Glen Jones	Emerald Green	*400
1980	Little Girls	Glen Jones	Emerald Green	*200
1980	Little Boys	Glen Jones	Emerald Green	*50
1980s	Rose	Hummelwerk	Ruby Red	**50
1980s	Unicorn	Hummelwerk	Emerald Green	**40
1980s	Unicorn	Hummelwerk	Cobalt Blue	**25

*Approximate number
**Number made for Hummelwerk. Being made in small numbers by Glen Jones.

At left, the 1977 Fischer Crystal frosted Christmas bell with a flying dove, made by using a deep abrasive etching process. 2-3/4"d. x 6"h.. $35-45. The same masked design was used for the 1980 bell in emerald green, at right. 2-1/2"d. x 7-1/4"h. $100-125.

Three Christmas bells by Fischer Crystal: 1978 "The Choir" in ruby red glass; 1979 "Nativity" in cobalt blue glass; and 1980 "Three Wise Men" in emerald green. 2-1/2"d. x 7"h. $75-100 ea.

Three Fischer Crystal bells: "Clipper Ship" in emerald green; "Star of David" in cobalt blue; and "Little Girls" in emerald green. 2-1/2"d. x 7-1/4"h., 1980. $100-125 ea.

Opposite page

Left: A Fischer Crystal bell with cameo profile of a little girl, issued in 1977 in a limited edition of 2,500. It is signed and serial numbered in very small letters in the scalloped decoration at the base of the handle. 3"d. x 6"h. $50-75. *Courtesy of Fischer Crystal Bells.*

Center: A Fischer Crystal bell, first edition of "A Bell for Mother" issued in 1975 as a limited edition of 5,000. 3"d. x 6"h. $35-50. *Courtesy of Fischer Crystal Bells.*

Right: A Fischer Crystal bell issued in 1975 as the first edition of a Christmas bell. 3"d. x 6"h. $35-50. *Courtesy of Fischer Crystal Bells.*

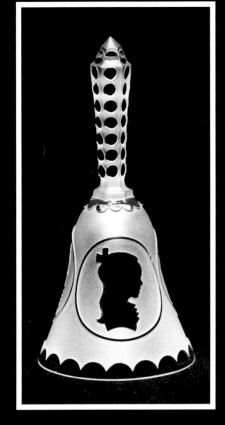

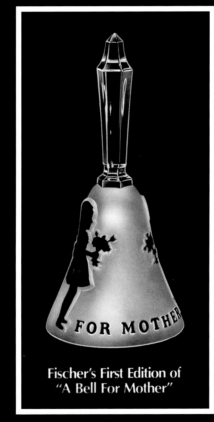

Fischer's First Edition of
"A Bell For Mother"

Fostoria Glass Company
Moundsville, West Virginia, 1891-1986

The Fostoria Glass Company produced pressed pattern glass and etched blown glass bells starting in 1977. They made bells for holidays and special events, including Christmas, Mother's Day, and weddings. They also made bells to match their stemware patterns. An example is the etched #338 Chintz bell. The best known pattern glass bell is the American line 2056, produced for less than eighteen months in 1981-82. One of the etched pattern glass bells most popular with collectors is the etched #327 Navarre pattern, produced in clear, blue, and pink. Fostoria made several special bells for Avon. Some of the company's ruby bells are signed with an "F". Lenox, Inc. acquired the Fostoria Glass Co. in the late 1980s.

A Fostoria Glass Co. bell made for Avon in 1979, in a ruby roman rosette design, "Cape Cod" pattern. 3-1/2"d. x 6-1/2"h. $20-25.

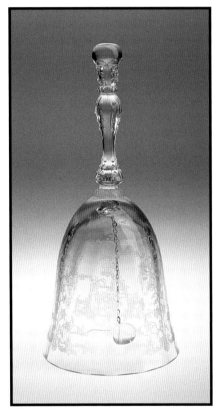

A Fostoria Glass Co. bell in an amethyst etched "Navarre" pattern. 3"d. x 6-1/2"h., c. 1977. $90-100.

A Fostoria glass bell in the "American, Line 2056" pattern. 1981-1982. $650-700. *Courtesy of Leslie Piña.*

A Fostoria Glass Co. bell in an amber "Serenity" etched pattern with clear multi-knop handle. 2-3/4"d. x 6-1/4"h. $30-40.

Guernsey Glass Company
Cambridge, Ohio, 1970-

The Guernsey Glass Company produces handmade reproduction glassware. Among bell collectors, the company is known for the glass bells produced using molds acquired in 1951 when the Akro Agate Company went out of business. The bells from these molds can be distinguished from the Akro Agate bells by two features; the Akro symbol of a flying crow holding two marbles has been replaced by a "B" for Harold Bennett (the owner of Guernsey Glass), and the base of the handle is rounded instead of having the six sides of the handle continue before meeting the shoulder of the bell. Some of the clear blue glass bells produced by Guernsey for the 1976 Bicentennial may still carry the Akro mark. Some bells can be found with a paper label.

A Guernsey Glass Co. "Smocking" pattern bell in a Cambridge Glass Co. Crown Tuscan color, with gold lettering for the Bicentennial along the rim. It has a paper label marked "Bennett." 3-1/4"d. x 5-1/2"h., c. 1976. $30-40.

Three Guernsey Glass Co. bells in a "Smocking" pattern made from Akro Agate molds in carnival blue, frosted, and clear blue with 1976 Bicentennial in gold letters. 3-1/4"d. x 5-1/2"h., c. 1970s. $20-25 ea.

Two Guernsey Glass Co. bells in a "Smocking" pattern, one in pink and white marble glass and one in chocolate and white marble glass. 3-1/4"d. x 5-1/2"h., c. 1980. $30-40 ea.

A. H. Heisey & Company
Newark, Ohio, 1896-1957

Heisey's engraved bells are presented in Chapter Four. In this chapter, two bells in the Victorian Belle pressed molded pattern are presented, one in clear glass and the other in frosted glass. The chain holding the clapper is inserted in a hole filled with plaster. When the Heisey company equipment was sold in 1958, the molds for these bells were sold to the Imperial Glass Company.

A series of Victorian Belle bells produced from Heisey molds by the Imperial Glass Co. and then by the Heisey Collectors of America. HCA had several glass companies use the molds to produce the bells in various colors of clear and frosted glass. 2-3/4"d. x 4-1/4"h., 1960-1999. $15-40 ea.

A pair of Heisey glass "Victorian Belle" bells in clear and frosted glass. 2-3/4"d. x 4-1/4"h., c. 1943. $75-100 ea.

Hobbs, Barnes and Company
Wheeling, West Virginia, 1849-1863

Hobbs, Brockunier and Company
Wheeling, West Virginia, 1863-1881

In the presidential election of 1860, Senators John Bell and Edward Everett from the Democratic southern conservative wing ran against Lincoln. The Hobbs company made bells that supporters of Bell and Everett used in a parade. The Oglebay Institute Glass Museum, Wheeling, West Virginia has one of these bells on display. It is one of the oldest American glass bells.

Heisey Collectors of America, Inc.
Newark, Ohio, 1974-

When the Imperial Glass Company declared bankruptcy in 1982, the molds for the Victorian Belle bell (which the company had acquired from A. H. Heisey & Company in 1958) were sold to the Heisey Collectors of America, Inc., which has a museum in Newark, Ohio. Since 1984, the museum has had various glass companies use the mold to reproduce the Victorian Belle bell in at least seven colors, both in clear glass and in frosted glass, and they have been sold by the museum at various times.

The logo on these bells varies, depending on the year they were made. Bells can be found marked with HCA, HCA86, HCA89, HCA95, and HCA96, as well as a D for Dalzell-Viking Glass Co. and IG or ALIG for the Imperial Glass Company. On these bells the chain holding the clapper is attached to two glass prongs, whereas the original Heisey Victorian Belle bells in colorless clear and frosted glass have the chain inserted into a hole filled with plaster.

A Hobbs, Barnes and Company clear blown glass bell engraved "1860/ Bell & Everett." Senator John Bell, a candidate for President, and his running mate, Edward Everett, from the southern conservative wing of the Democratic Party, were opponents of Abraham Lincoln in the Presidential election of 1860. The bell was carried by supporters of Bell and Everett in a parade. Plaster of paris fills the handle to hold the clapper. *Courtesy of the Collection of the Museums of Oglebay Institute, Wheeling, WV.*

Imperial Glass Corporation
Bellaire, Ohio, 1901-1984

The Imperial Glass Corporation started as the Imperial Glass Company, but was reorganized in 1931 as a corporation. Lenox, Inc. purchased the company in 1973 and it continued operations under Lenox until 1981 when the company was sold to Arthur Lorch. In 1982, the company was purchased by Robert Stahl, but it did not prosper and it filed for bankruptcy in 1984.

In the 1950s, the company used superimposed letters I and G on some of its glass. After Lenox purchased the company, an L was added to the IG. Briefly, while Arthur Lorch controlled the company, an A was added to the LIG. During its final years, some glass was made with initials NI for New Imperial. Upon the liquidation of the company, molds were sold to the Heisey Collectors of America, the National Cambridge Collectors Club, and other glass companies. The Santa Christmas bell mold was sold to Boyd's Crystal Art Glass Co. Bells can be found with any of the above noted combinations of initials.

In 1957, Imperial made clear, colored, blown glass bells with hollow handles which used a cork to support a clear crystal clapper.

Some favorite Imperial glass bells among collectors are those of slag or marbled glass produced in four colors. These were produced between 1959 and 1977, in mold #720, in a glossy and satin finish. No two bells are alike, as the mixture of milk white and colored glass varies considerably. The ruby slag varies from a deep red to an orange-yellow. The jade slag varies from a dark green to a light turquoise, and the caramel slag varies from a light to dark brown. The purple slag appears to be the most consistent in color. The molds for these bells are the same as those used for Imperial's clear glass bells in the early 1930s colored in green and rose. After 1973, some paper labels have a computer number 43842 used by Lenox. Upon the liquidation of Imperial in 1984, the molds for these bells were sold to Boyd's Crystal Art Glass Company.

Four Imperial Glass bells of slag glass, mold 720, glossy finish, in ruby, purple, caramel, and jade. Generally, the chain supporting the glass bead clapper is attached to an eye screw embedded in the glass. Some bells are found with glass prongs holding the chain. 3"d. x 5-1/2"h., 1959-1977. $40-55 ea.

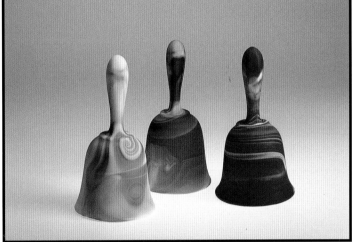

Three Imperial Glass bells of satin finish slag glass, mold 720, in green, caramel, and ruby. Purple is also found. 3"d. x 5-1/2"h., 1959-1977. $40-55 ea.

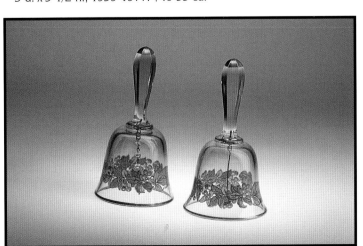

Two Imperial Glass bells in clear pink and green glass decorated with a vintage design and gold trim. 3"d. x 5-1/2"h., c. 1930. $40-60 ea.

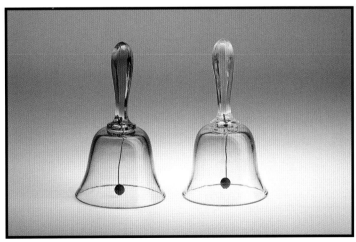

Imperial Glass clear pink and green glass bells. Same mold 720 as used for the later bells. Clappers are clear glass beads supported on a thin chain. The chain is attached to the glass by an eye screw embedded in the glass. 3"d. x 5-1/2"h., c. 1930s. $25-40 ea.

Clear pink Imperial Glass bells with floral and geometric painted decorations. 3"d. x 5-1/2"h., c. 1930. $30-40 ea.

Four Imperial Glass "Colonial" bells with hollow handles holding a cork to support a teardrop clapper, c. 1957. Left to right: Ruby, 4"d. x 7-1/2"h.; Burgundy, 4"d. x 7-1/2"h.; Stiegel Green, 4-1/4"d. x 6-3/4"h.; Antique Blue, 3-3/4"d. x 7-1/4"h. $50-75 ea.

An Imperial Glass bell in pink clear glass decorated with a band of black and gold flowers along the rim. 3"d. x 5-1/2"h., c. 1930. $20-30.

An Imperial Glass lemon frost "Suzanne" bell. The bell has Imperial Glass logo "I" superimposed on "N" for New Imperial. 3-1/4"d. x 5"h., c. 1983. $35-50.

Clear sky blue Imperial Glass Santa bell, made for Mary C. Walrath (an independent distributor) and signed by her. It has the superimposed N and I for "New Imperial," #187/200. 3-3/4"d. x 6-1/4"h., 1983. $45-55.

Jefferson Glass Company
Follansbee, West Virginia, 1907-1930

Between 1910 and 1915, the Jefferson Glass Company produced glass bells with a wide gold band along the outside edge of a raised rim. The mold for the bell originated with the Ohio Flint Glass Company of Lancaster, Ohio as part of their Chippendale pattern glassware patented on February 5, 1907. The Jefferson Glass Company obtained the patent rights to the mold in 1908 when the Ohio Flint Glass Company went out of business.

The bell was produced as a souvenir item in three basic colors: custard glass and ruby flashed glass, both with a gold band, and a marigold carnival glass. A variation of the custard glass is a translucent greenish yellow glass similar to vaseline glass.

The Jefferson Glass Company sold the molds to the Central Glass Works in 1919 and that company produced the bell in clear glass.

All of the bells have an eye screw embedded in the glass to hold a stiff wire and lead ball clapper. They have a tapered hexagonal handle which is clear on the ruby flashed and carnival glass bells.

As is typical of many Jefferson Glass items, most of the custard bells have a characteristic rose decoration. Although the bells with the rose were made by Jefferson, the souvenir inscription was applied by others. Prices on the bells vary depending on the condition of the gold band and other decoration.

Left: Jefferson Glass Co. bells in ruby flashed glass with gold trim and advertising, clear handle. Left to right: Niagara Falls, Kaiserhof 1911-1912, and Coney Island. 3-1/4"d. x 6-1/4"h. $50-90 ea.

Right: A Jefferson Glass Co. bell in amber carnival glass, clear handle, with etched "Souvenir Glencoe, Minn." 3-1/4"d. x 6-1/4"h. $60-80.

Left: A custard glass Jefferson Glass Co. bell decorated with a seal for "Annual Convention S. C., Beaver Falls, May 1, 1911." On the reverse side, another seal states "Souvenir, Fall City Council, O.U.A.M., 385" with a flag and compass. Inside, in red lettering, is the name of the decorating company: A.G. Spec. Co., Monaca, Pa. 3-1/4"d. x 6-1/4"h. $50-60. This bell can also be found with an oak handle, 7" tall.

Right: Jefferson Glass Co. bells in custard glass with gold rim and painted rose typical of these bells. Center bell has advertising of "H.B. 1915" (Hotel Biltmore) and bell on right advertises "Tennanah Lake, N. Y." 3-1/4"d. x 6-1/4"h., c. 1915. $60-80 ea.

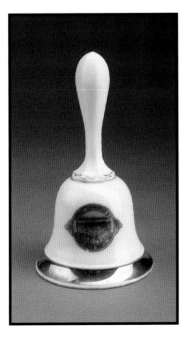 

Lenox, Inc.
Lawrenceville, New Jersey, 1980s–

Lenox has produced glass bells with frosted or china figural handles, including some with Disney characters, and some for celebration of holidays and special events. Some of their bells have been produced from molds acquired from other glass companies which have gone out of business, such as Imperial and Fostoria.

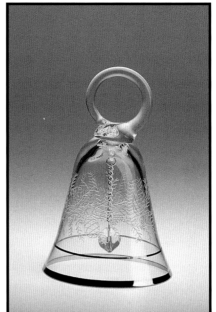

A clear Lenox Crystal Co. bell with etched pine cones and silver trimming, ring handle. Some are signed Lenox with a date. 2-1/4"d. x 3-1/2"h., c. 1980s. $20-30.

A clear Lenox Crystal Co. bell for Disney with a ceramic Mickey Mouse handle. 2-3/4"d. x 5-3/4"h., dated 1997. $25-35.

A clear Lenox Crystal Co. bell with a gold rim and a frosted Santa handle, signed Lenox 1985. 3-3/4"d. x 7-1/2"h. $30-40.

Libbey Glass Company
Toledo, Ohio, 1892-

At the World's Columbian Exposition of 1893 in Chicago, Illinois, the Libbey Glass Company had a complete glass factory able to produce many types of glass products. Among the souvenir glass items available to those attending the Libbey exhibit was a series of blown etched bells with twisted, pressed glass handles. Another souvenir was a pressed glass, bell shaped container, which was a glass replica of the first bell rung in the New World — brought by Columbus on his second voyage in 1493. The original bronze bell was on loan to the 1893 fair. The importance of this glass replica is that it provides evidence which supports that Libbey made the etched bells. The lettering on the replica states that it was made by Libbey Glass Co., Toledo, Ohio and it has misspellings which are reflected in the lettering on the shoulders of some of the etched bells: the word "exposition" has the second "i" missing and the "n" is reversed.

The etched bells have a chain with a hollow ball clapper attached to a loop in a twisted wire embedded in the glass. Each has a star impressed on the top of its handle. Some of these bells were etched with the name or initials of a fair attendee.

Two variations of the Libbey Glass Co. bell from the 1893 Columbian Exposition with dashed circles surrounding the etched "Worlds Fair 1893." The bell on the right does not have molded wording along the shoulder. 3"d. x 4-1/4"h. $150-175 ea.

Left: A Libbey Glass Co. pressed glass, bell shaped candy container issued for the 1893 World's Columbian Exposition in Chicago. It helps to identify the etched glass bells produced by Libbey at their factory on the World's Fair site. Along the edge is molded "Worlds Columbia Expositon. Libbey Glass Co., Toledo, Ohio." The missing second "i" and reverse "n" in "Exposition" is reflected in the lettering on the etched bells. 3"d. x 5"h. $60-75.

Right: A Libbey Glass Co. bell from the 1893 World's Columbian Exposition etched with "Worlds Fair 1893" in a circle with banners and flowers flanking the circle. Molded on the shoulder of the bell is "1893 Worlds Columbian Expositon" with a reverse "n" in "Columbian" and the second "i" missing in "Exposition." The frosted handle has a star molded at the top. 3"d. x 4-1/4"h. $150-175.

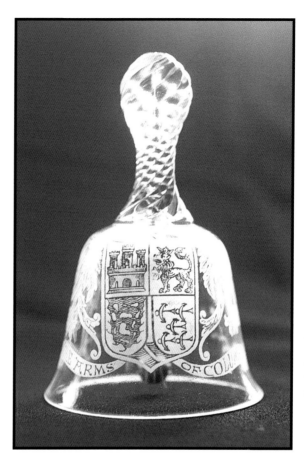

Left: A Libbey Glass Co. bell from the 1893 Columbian Exposition with an etched scene of the landing of Columbus. On the other side is an etching of Columbus' three ships and natives running into the woods. Note that there is no molded lettering on the shoulder of the bell. 3"d. x 4-1/4"h. $200-250.

Right: A Libbey Glass Co. bell from the 1893 Columbian Exposition etched with the coat of arms of Columbus, clear handle. There is no molded lettering on the shoulder of the bell. This bell can be found also with a frosted handle. 3"d. x 4-1/4"h. $200-250.

Left: A clear glass Libbey Glass Co. bell etched with "Worlds Fair 1893." No embossed lettering. 3"d. x 4-1/4"h. $150-175.

Right: A Libbey Glass Co. bell with someone's initials etched at the Libbey Glass factory at the 1893 Columbian Exposition, Chicago. 3"d. x 4-1/4"h. $125-150.

The Lotus Glass Company, Inc.
Barnesville, Ohio, 1912–

The Lotus Glass Company started in 1912 as the Lotus Cut Glass Company, but the name was changed to the Lotus Company in the 1920s. Lotus produced a large variety of hand decorated glass bells from blanks made by Bryce Brothers, Cambridge, Central, Duncan & Miller, Fostoria, Heisey, Seneca, and other glass producers. No glassware has been made at Lotus; they only decorated glass. Some of their bells have beautiful finishes. Until about 1980, some bells were encrusted with 22 karat gold, silver, or platinum. Others have delicate, acid etched designs. Some bells can be found with a Lotus paper label attached.

A pair of Lotus Glass Co. bells etched in "Bridal Bouquet" pattern, one in gold. 2-3/4"d. x 4-3/4"h., c. 1930. $40-50 ea.

A pair of Lotus Glass Co. bells etched in the "Georgian" pattern with applied gold, stem #98. 3"d. x 4-1/2"h., $30-40 ea.

Lotus Glass Co. bells in "Virginian," clear, and "Colonial" patterns. 3"d. x 4-3/4"h., 1965-77. $25-35 ea.

Lotus Glass Co. bells in pale amber iridescent glass, "Vesta." and "Sovereign" patterns on stem #1041 having handles with three knops. 2-3/4"d. x 5"h. $20-25 ea.

Lotus Glass Co. bells in "Hostess" pattern, 2-3/4"d. x 5-1/2"h., and "Georgian" pattern, 2-1/2"d x 4-3/4"h., c. 1967. $20-25 ea.

A paper label found on Lotus bells.

Maslach Art Glass
Greenbrae, California, 1971–

Steven Maslach, working at his Cuneo Furnace, has become well known in the art glass world for his marbles. He has also made art glass bells, sought by collectors of his glass as well as by bell collectors. The bells seen by the author are signed and dated along the inside edge.

A Maslach Art Glass bell in iridescent antique gold on a swirled bowl with a clear knurled handle. It is signed on the inside edge with *Maslach 6-80*. Bells are also known in iridescent cobalt glass. 3"d. x 5-3/4"h., c. 1980. $80-90.

Mosser Glass, Inc.
Cambridge, Ohio, 1971–

Mosser Glass produces reproductions of various glassware including bells.

Two Mosser Glass bells in a "Daisy & Button" pattern and an "M" in a circle. Made in five colors. 3"d. x 5-1/4"h., c. 1976. $20-25 ea.

McKee Glass Company
Jeannette, Pennsylvania, 1908–1951

The McKee Glass Co. started operations as McKee and Brothers Glass Works in 1853, originally in Pittsburgh, Pennsylvania. The firm moved to Jeanette, Pennsylvania about 1888. The company started producing pressed glass items in imitation of cut glass in 1904, calling them PRESCUT in a series of patterns. The only bells produced by the company known to the author are in the "Yutec" pattern, made from 1901 to about 1915.

Three pressed glass Bicentennial Liberty Bells from the Mosser Glass Co., one in clear glass and two in carnival glass, signed with an "M" in a circle. 2-3/4"d. x 6"h. $20-25 ea.

Two early molded "Yutec" pattern bells by McKee Glass Co. in clear glass. The left bell is amethyst in color from exposure to sunlight. Heavy iron chain and clapper is supported by two glass prongs. Some of these bells have an advertisement molded along the rim reading "Compliments of the Rubel Furniture Company." 2-1/4"d. x 5"h., c. 1920s. $25-35 ea.

Mount Washington Glass Company
New Bedford, Massachusetts, 1869-1900

From about 1876 until 1894, when it merged with the Pairpoint Manufacturing Company, the Mount Washington Glass Company produced several blown molded glass bells. White lusterless glass, also known as Lusterless White or Opal Satin, was the first art glass produced by the company. The name refers to the satin finish of the glass, which had been given a hydrofluoric acid bath resulting in a smooth, white, alabaster type appearance.

An opal satin bell is illustrated in a Mount Washington catalog Appointments page from about 1895-1900. These small opal satin bells with a twisted handle can be found with colorful painted flowers. The clappers are made of solid silver on a chain attached to the glass via the wire loop of an embedded twisted iron wire.

Bells in the satin or lustrous opal finish, as well as in clear glass, are known molded in the shape of a Liberty Bell with a handle in the form of a chain. These bells can be found painted with flowers or with gold decoration. All have a very small molded 1776 along the edge of the shoulder. Most of the bells have a long brass chain and bullet shaped brass clapper. Some may be found with a hollow, two part clapper and chain typical of late nineteenth century and early twentieth century American glass bells.

A Mount Washington Glass Co. bell in lusterless white or opal satin finish painted with blue flowers and gold decoration on a twisted handle. The silver chain with solid clapper is attached to a loop on an embedded twisted wire. 3-1/4"d. x 4-1/2"h., c. 1895. $200-250.

Three Mount Washington Glass Co. bells in opal glass with chain design handle, some with gold decoration. All have a long brass chain and clapper. The left hand bell has a satin finish, the other two are in a lustrous white. Small molded 1776 on edge of shoulder. 3-1/2"d. x 5"h., c. 1900. $150-200 ea.

A Mount Washington Glass Co. bell in opal satin finish with painted flowers and gold decoration, with chain design handle and a brass chain and clapper. Small molded 1776 along edge of shoulder. 3-1/2"d. x 5"h., c. 1900. $200-300. *Courtesy of Sally & Rob Roy.*

A Mount Washington Glass Co. bell in a lustrous white finish painted with a wild rose, with chain design handle and a brass chain and clapper. Small molded 1776 along edge of shoulder. 3-1/2"d. x 5"h., c. 1900. $200-300.

A Mount Washington Glass Co. bell in an opal satin finish with gold and floral decoration and chain design handle. Small molded 1776 along edge of shoulder. 3-1/2"d. x 5"h., c. 1900. $250-300.

A Mt. Washington Glass Co. bell in clear glass with gold bands and painted flowers, chain design handle. It was issued as a souvenir of Roscoe-Rockland in New York State. The bell has a hollow two part clapper and chain and there is a small molded 1776 along the edge of shoulder. 3-1/4"d. x 5-1/4"h., c. 1900. $200-250.

Clear glass bells with a twisted handle can be found with painted flowers. The paint has flaked off on many of these bells. The author believes these were made by Mount Washington in a glass similar to their Verona glass, a clear glass decorated only on the outside. The clappers are hollow two piece balls on a thin chain, attached to the loop of an embedded twisted iron wire or on a chain set in a hole filled with plaster. Some of these bells were made as souvenirs for the 1893 Columbian Exposition in Chicago, Illinois.

The author believes these to be Mount Washington Glass Co. bells. They are in clear glass with painted flowers or gold decoration, and a twisted handle. The chain is attached to a loop on an embedded twisted wire or embedded in a hole in the glass filled with plaster. The center bell is painted with "Columbian Souvenir 1893." Left to right: 3"d. x 4-3/4"h.; 3"d. x 4-1/4"h.; 3"d. x 5"h.; 3"d. x 4-1/4"h.; and 3-3/4"d. x 4-3/4"h. $40-60 ea.

Pairpoint Crystal Company, Inc.
Sagamore, Massachusetts, 1970–

The Pairpoint Manufacturing Company was established in 1880 in New Bedford, Massachusetts, and merged with the Mount Washington Glass Company in 1894 to form the Pairpoint Corporation. In 1938, the company was sold to a salvage company, which resold the company to a New Bedford, Massachusetts group to form the Gundersen Glass Works with Robert Gundersen as manager. In 1952, the company became part of the National Pairpoint Company and was known as the Gundersen-Pairpoint Glass Works. A few years later, in 1957, Robert Bryden became manager of the firm under the name Pairpoint Glass Company, Inc. Under Bryden, the firm leased facilities in Spain from 1958 until 1970 when it moved to Sagamore, Massachusetts. The firm was sold to Robert Bancroft in 1988 and the name was changed to Pairpoint Crystal Co., Inc. in 1993. Pairpoint was subsequently sold to Valerie Kelly in 1998 and con-

tinues today under the name of Pairpoint Crystal Company, Inc.

While some bells were made in the 1920s in clear glass and engraved with grapes, the company is known for the beautiful glass bells produced since 1970. In the late 1990s, some engraved bells were made with artistic handles and colorful rims. Most Pairpoint bells are signed with a P in a diamond. Many have been painted with flowers and various scenes.

Clappers are generally made of glass, occasionally as a prism, and attached to the bell by a metallic, seven point star; note that a six point star with rounded ends has been used on a few bells. On large bells that have the handle of the bell inserted in a collar at the top of the bell body, the two are joined by plaster and the clapper is held by a wire that has been inserted into the base of the handle. Since the late 1990s, the handles of large bells have been bonded to the body of the bell by an adhesive.

A Pairpoint Collectors Club was formed in 1995 and the company has made at least one bell for members each year.

A clear green Pairpoint Glass Co. bell with embedded twisted iron wire to support a replaced wire and iron clapper. Also known decorated with grapes. 3"d. x 6-1/4"h., 1920-1930. $60-80.

Four Pairpoint bells in teal glass with painted decorations, c. 1980s. Left to right: flowers and bee, 3-1/2"d. x 6-1/2"h.; flowers and butterfly, 3-3/4"d. x 6-3/4"h.; birds, 4"d. x 7"h.; and flowers, 3-3/4"d. x 7"h. $50-70 ea.

Two variations of the first edition of 200 bells from a series of annual bells, in a cased glass of white over pink called "Peach Blow" by Pairpoint. The left bell is opaque with painted flowers and a clear six knop handle encasing a pink and white twisted glass ribbon. 4-1/2"d. x 10-3/4"h. The right bell is translucent with painted flowers, and has a clear six knop handle encasing a green and white twisted glass ribbon. 4-3/4"d. x 11-1/2"h. 1974. $300-350 ea.

The third edition of 100 bells from a series of annual bells by Pairpoint, in an amethyst colored glass decorated with flowers. Clear seven knop handle with a twisted white ribbon. 5"d. x 12-1/2"h., 1976. $275-325.

The second edition of 100 bells from a series of annual bells by Pairpoint, in a decorated French Blue glass. Clear handle with a twisted white ribbon and six knops. 4-1/2"d. x 12"h., 1975. $350-400.

The fourth edition of 100 bells from a series of annual bells by Pairpoint, in an emerald green glass with painted flowers. Clear six knop handle with a twisted white ribbon. 4-3/4"d. x 12-1/4"h., 1977. $275-325.

The fifth edition of 100 bells from a series of annual bells by Pairpoint, in cobalt blue glass with painted flowers. Clear three knop handle with twisted white ribbon. 5"d. x 11-1/2"h., 1978. $275-325.

The sixth edition of 100 bells from a series of annual bells by Pairpoint, in violet glass painted with flowers. Clear five knop handle with twisted white ribbon. 5"d. x 11-1/2"h., 1979. $275-325.

The seventh and last edition of 100 bells from the annual series by Pairpoint, in a teal glass painted with flowers. Clear four knop handle with twisted white ribbon. 4-3/4"d. x 11-1/2"h., 1980. $250-300.

Left: A Pairpoint bell in a mottled glass, clear six knop handle with a twisted red and white glass ribbon. 5"d. x 12-1/4"h., c. 1980s. $275-325.

Right: A Pairpoint bell in cobalt blue with swirled ribbing and a clear rounded handle. Signed D. McDermott, 1987. 5-1/2"d. x 9-1/2"h. $175-225.

Three Pairpoint bells with spiral striping, 1990s. Left to right: clear with black and violet striping, 3-1/4"d. x 6-1/2"h., $125-175; cobalt blue with white striping and four knop clear handle with twisted white ribbon, 5"d. x 9-3/4"h., $225-275; clear with white striping, 5"d. x 8-1/4"h., $100-150.

Three Pairpoint bells with spiral striping, 1990s. Left to right: aqua green with white chevron striping and clear handle, 3-1/4"d. x 6-1/2"h., $90-110; cobalt blue with white striping and three knop handle, 3"d. x 5-3/4"h., $80-100; clear green with white striping and clear handle, 3-1/2"d. x 6-3/4"h., $75-95.

Three Pairpoint bells with Nailsea type loops, 1980s-1990s. Left to right: cobalt blue with white loops, 3"d. x 6"h., $110-150; cranberry with white loops and clear five knop handle with twisted white ribbon, 4-3/4"d. x 10-3/4"h., $250-300; cased blue on white glass showing white loops and clear one knop handle, 4"d. x 7-3/4"h., $100-125.

Three Pairpoint bells with quilted pattern and clear handles, 1990s. Left to right: blue, 3-3/4"d. x 6-3/4"h., $60-75; green, 3-3/4"d. x 6-3/4"h., $45-60; violet with painted flowers, 4"d. x 7-1/2"h., $80-100.

Two Pairpoint bells with cobalt blue handles and rims, 1990s. Clear bell on the left, 3-3/4"d. x 7"h.; clear swirled pattern bell on the right, 3-1/4"d. x 7"h. $60-80 ea.

A variety of teal Pairpoint bells, 1990s. Left to right: clear handle, 2-3/4"d. x 5"h.; three knop handle with painted daisy, 2-1/2"d. x 4-1/2"h.; clear teal, 2-3/4"d. x 6"h.; and painted with violets, 2-1/2"d. x 4-3/4"h. $40-70 ea.

A Pairpoint bell with mottled blue and green ribbing and a three knop handle. 4-1/4"d. x 8"h. $110-125.

Three Pairpoint bells in cased glass, color over white, c. 1980s. Left to right: teal with painted Christmas scene, 3-3/4"d. x 7"h.; caramel with white handle and amber clapper, 3-1/2"d. x 7"h.; teal with painted floral rim, 3-3/4"d. x 7-1/4"h. $100-140 ea.

A Pairpoint bell issued for the Bicentennial in clear glass with engraved eagle and two stars, blue handle separated by a clear glass ball, one of 500. 5-1/4"d. x 10"h., 1976. $175-200.

A Pairpoint bell issued for the Collectors' Club in 1996, engraved on clear glass with the Barrington-Mayfair design produced by Robert Mason and David McDermott. Air twist handle and cobalt blue rim. 5-1/2"d. x 10-1/2"h. $250-300.

Two Pairpoint
bells issued for
the Pairpoint
Collectors'
Club, in clear
glass with
colored flower
in glass ball at
base of handle.
4-1/4"d. x
9-1/4"h., 1995.
$150-175 ea.

Three Pairpoint bells issued in 1997 for the Collectors' Club, in opalescent glass with an iridescent finish created by glass blowers Robert Mason and David McDermott. Left to right: blue with painted flowers, 3"d. x 6-1/2"h., $140-160; plain, 3"d. x 6"h., $100-120; light blue with floral rim and butterfly, 3"d. x 6"h., $130-150.

A Pairpoint bell with a blue and pink swirled pattern, four knop handle, and twisted white glass ribbon made in 1999 for the Pairpoint Collector's Club. 5-1/4"d. x 11"h. $200-225.

Left: an iridescent amethyst glass Pairpoint bell with a five knop clear handle and twisted white ribbon, made for the 1998 Collector's Club. 5"d. x 12"h. $210-230. Right: a clear green bell painted with a winter scene. 5-3/4"d. x 12"h. $215-235. Note that the glass sleeve into which the handle usually fits has been replaced by a flat disk in these later bells.

Left: A Pilgrim Glass bell with sand carved "Ebony Stampede" cameo design of black running horses over mocha colored cased glass. Signed K/P 1999, for Kelsey Murphy and Pilgrim, register no. 913154. 3-3/4"d. x 7-1/2"h. $200-250.

Right: A Pilgrim cameo glass bell, sand carved in a "Lavender Iris" pattern in lavender over mocha colored cased glass. Signed on the top of handle with K/P 2000 and registry no. 913156. 4"d. x 8"h. $200-250.

Left: A Pilgrim cameo glass bell, sand carved in "Mocha Dolphin" pattern in blue over mocha colored cased glass. Signed on inside rim with Kelsey/Pilgrim 1999 and registry no. 913152. 3-3/4"d. x 7-3/4"h. $200-250.

Right: A Pilgrim cameo glass bell, sand carved in "Cranberry Gardens" pattern in red over mocha colored cased glass. Signed on top of handle with K/P 1999 and registry no. 913151. 4"d. x 7-3/4"h. $200-250.

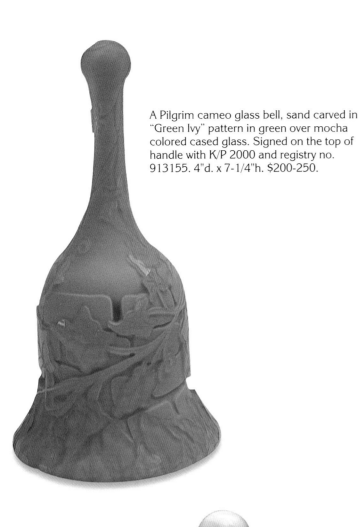

A Pilgrim cameo glass bell, sand carved in "Green Ivy" pattern in green over mocha colored cased glass. Signed on the top of handle with K/P 2000 and registry no. 913155. 4"d. x 7-1/4"h. $200-250.

St. Clair produced several glass bells to commemorate special events. Their glass bell paperweights are popular amongst collectors.

A St. Clair Glass Works bell in cobalt blue carnival glass issued for the Bicentennial. Molded with fruit, 1776-1976, 200 years, and Joe St. Clair. 4"d. x 7"h. $80-100.

A Pilgrim cameo glass bell, sand carved in "Yellow Rose" pattern in yellow over mocha colored cased glass. Signed on the top of handle with K/P and registry no. 913153. 4"d. x 7-1/4"h. $200-250.

A St. Clair Glass Works bell in cobalt blue carnival molded for the American Carnival Glass Association, Tenth Annual Convention, Dayton, Ohio, July 4, 1975. Also shows Carillon Bell Tower, and J.ST.C. 4-1/4"d. x 7"h. $100-120.

A St. Clair Glass Works bell in chocolate glass with a "Roman Rosette" pattern. 3"d. x 6"h., 1982. $60-70.

A St. Clair Glass Works Bicentennial bell paperweight in green Carnival glass with 1776 and 1976 molded on opposite sides. Joe St. Clair is molded on the top inside the bell. This bell can be found in many colors. 2-1/4"d. x 3"h. $25-35.

L. E. Smith Glass Co.

Mt. Pleasant, Pennsylvania, 1907–

L. E. Smith, a subsidiary of Owens-Illinois, Inc., has reproduced early American pattern glassware items, including bells in the "Moon and Star" pattern. The bell is known in ten or more colors produced since 1979.

An L. E. Smith Glass Co. ruby carnival glass bell in the "Moon and Star" pattern. The bell in this pattern is known in at least ten colors. 3"d. x 6"h. $25-35.

Steuben Glass Works

Corning, New York, 1903-1936

During the time that Frederick Carder was actively designing and producing various glassware at Steuben, some bells were made. In 1918, the company was acquired by the Corning Glass Works and became its Art Glass Division, primarily under the direction of Frederick Carder. Herein is presented a bell made before 1933 in Selenium Ruby.

In 1933, Steuben Glass, Inc. was formed and it produced many items, including bells. Between 1936 and 1962, four bells were made in the clear crystal for which Steuben became famous.

A Frederick Carder Steuben bell in Selenium Ruby with a clear handle, c. 1920. 3-1/4"d. x 5-3/4"h. $200-250.

Four Steuben Glass Works bells in clear crystal. Left to right: #8139 by Lloyd Atkins, 2-1/2"d. x 4-1/2"h., 1962, $180-200; #7813 by Samuel Ayres, 2-1/4"d. x 3-1/2"h., 1938, $140-160; #7986 by Jeanne Leach, 1-1/2"d. x 6"h., air twist handle, signed clapper, 1949, $400-450; #7768, fluted with octagonal fluted handle, 2"d. x 3-1/2"h., 1936, $150-170.

Summit Art Glass Co.
Rootstown, Ohio, 1972-

The Summit Art Glass Co. has produced glass bells primarily from molds acquired from companies that have ceased operations. Some bells have the impressed symbol of a "V" in a circle — for owner Russ Vogelsong — occasionally followed by the initials "SB". Sometimes a paper label is found; it is shaped like a hand and bears the notation "Hand pressed, made in U.S.A." plus the company name.

Two Summit Art Glass bells in chocolate glass, both in a "Wildflower" pattern but with different handles. The bell on the right has a hand shaped paper label. The same pattern has been made in other colors. 3-1/4"d. x 6"h. $30-40 ea.

A Summit Art Glass "Melanie" Colonial Belle in a purple slag. It has a "V" in a circle and "SB" along the outside rim. This bell has been made in many colors. 2-3/4"d. x 5-1/4"h. $50-60.

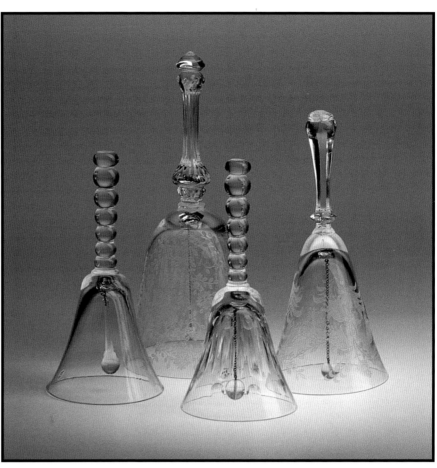

Tiffin Glass Co.
Tiffin, Ohio, 1888-1984

Tiffin glassware was produced under many owners. Since the day it opened, the plant produced stemware in hundreds of patterns and bells were made to match the large variety of stemware. Over the years the company produced many glass blanks, but it also bought molds from many other glass companies that had gone out of business, including Heisey, Duncan & Miller, and Hawkes. Tiffin produced primarily etched and cut glass bells, mostly on very thin glass; however, some pressed glass stemware was produced and bells may have also been made of pressed glass. Tiffin bells are best identified by a gold colored Tiffin label showing a "T" and the name on a shield. This label was used on glassware from 1916 to 1977. Between 1962 and 1980, some stemware was signed "Tiffin." Lacking a label or signature, many bells can be identified by matching their patterns with stemware patterns shown in various books on Tiffin glass.

Four Tiffin Glass bells, 1970s-1980s. Left to right: clear with seven knop handle, 2-3/4"d. x 5-3/4"h.; etched "June Night" pattern, stem 17392, 3-1/2"d. x 8"h.; cut pattern with seven knop handle, 2-3/4"d. x 5-3/4"h.; and etched "Fuchsia" pattern, 3"d. x 6-1/2"h. $30-60 ea.

A paper label found on Tiffin bells.

United States Glass Company
Pittsburgh, Pennsylvania, 1891-1930s

The United States Glass Co. was formed on July 1, 1891 as a merger of eighteen glass factories. Bells were produced by many of the individual companies, but a Liberty Bell in glass was made under the United States Glass Co. name in 1893 for the Columbian Exposition. Similar Liberty bells were made by the Mt. Washington Glass Co.

Two Viking Glass Co. ruby bells, one with "Georgian" pattern and one with "Arlington" pattern. 3-1/2"d. x 5-3/4"h., 1982. $25-30 ea.

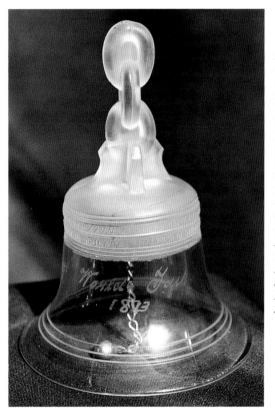

A United States Glass Co. Liberty Bell issued for the 1893 Columbian Exposition in Chicago, Illinois. The reverse side of the bell has July 4, 1776 engraved. *Courtesy of the Miller Collection: Joe, Francis, and Jim Miller, Harrison, Arkansas.*

Viking Glass Company
New Martinsville, West Virginia,
1944-1986

The Viking Glass Company started as the New Martinsville Glass Manufacturing Company in 1900, and changed owners in 1938 to become the New Martinsville Glass Company. In 1944, that company was sold and the new owners named it the Viking Glass Company. In 1986, the company was sold to Kenneth Dalzell and the name was changed to Dalzell-Viking Glass Company. Viking bells are known in ruby glass in five patterns, a "leaf" pattern in six colors, and a clear or frosted bell decorated with flowers, butterflies, and children, all produced in the 1980s.

A Viking Glass Co. ruby pressed glass bell in the "Yesteryear" pattern. 2-1/2"d. x 4"h. $20-30.

L. G. Wright Glass Co. bells in "Currier & Ives" pattern, ribbed handle and acorn top, in clear, amber, and blue. 4"d. x 6-3/4"h. and 2-3/4"d. x 5"h., 1970s. $25-45 ea.

This category includes bells made by glass firms for other companies.

Two gold rimmed clear glass bells from a series made by Sasaki Crystal in Japan for the Danbury Mint: swan handle, 1980 and floral handle, 1981. 3-3/4"d. x 7-3/4"h. $40-50 ea.

An American Bell Association 1998 St. Paul, Minnesota Convention bell designed by Marvin W. Dynes. Tom Reddy of the Reddy Glass Company, St. Paul, Minnesota, fabricated the bell; Robert Guenter, of Glass Art Design, Inc., Minneapolis, Minnesota, designed and applied the "Loon" and 1998 ABA Saint Paul, MN etching. The clapper is a Swarovski blue crystal suspended on a nickel chain. 2-1/2"d. x 4-1/2"h. $40-50.

An L. G. Wright Glass Co. bell in a clear "Frosted Leaf" pattern, with ribbed handle and acorn top. 4"d. x 6"h. $30-40.

American Blown and Pressed Glass Bells of Unknown Origin

Here are some bells believed to be of American origin, but the manufacturer is not known to the author.

A clear blown bell with a molded clear green flower handle. 3-1/2"d. 5-1/2"h. $30-35.

A Nailsea type clear aqua bell with white stripes. 2-3/4"d. x 7-1/2"h. c. 1970s. $30-40.

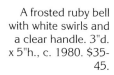

A frosted ruby bell with white swirls and a clear handle. 3"d. x 5"h., c. 1980. $35-45.

An amethyst to gold iridescent bell with a multifaceted clear top of handle. A souvenir of San Francisco. 2-1/2"d. x 5-1/2"h. $30-40.

Assorted flamework
glass bells from
various sources.
$15-40 ea.

Two clear glass bells with hollow handles. The bell on the right has gold decoration and red, white, and blue threads on the inside of its handle. Chain and clapper are bronze. 2-1/2"d. x 5-1/2"h., c. 1920s. $25-40 ea.

Kewpie doll bells. The two bells in the front have sharply defined fingers and the chain holding the clapper is held by two glass prongs. The author believes these two may have been made by Westmoreland as the dolls match known Westmoreland Kewpie doll articles of the same size. The three bells in the rear have ill defined fingers and the chain is supported by a plastic disk. These are reproductions from an Asian country. 2-1/4"d. x 5-1/2"h. $15-25 ea.

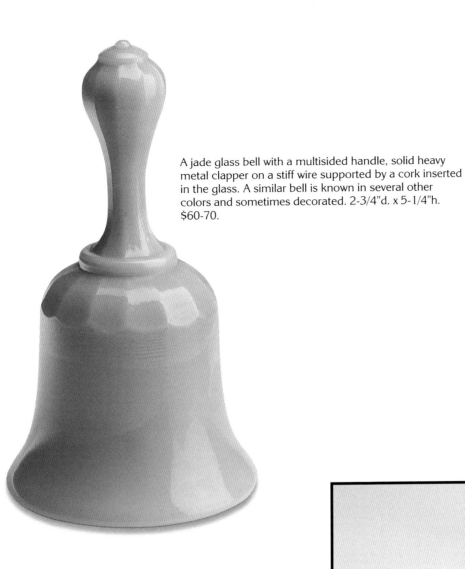

A jade glass bell with a multisided handle, solid heavy metal clapper on a stiff wire supported by a cork inserted in the glass. A similar bell is known in several other colors and sometimes decorated. 2-3/4"d. x 5-1/4"h. $60-70.

A ruby flashed glass bell with clear handle, replaced clapper. Engraved "Watertown, Wis., 1919." Flashing and time period is similar to ruby flashed Jefferson Glass Co. bells. 3"d. x 4-1/2"h. $200-225.

A clear glass bell with a "thousand eye" pattern and a wooden handle. The clapper is a clear, 1-1/2" diameter amber glass ball on a stiff wire. The thousand eye pattern was first made by Adams & Co., Pittsburgh, Pennsylvania, in the 1870s and by Richards & Hartley, Tarentum, Pennsylvania, in the 1880s. It was reproduced by Viking Glass Co. and Westmoreland Glass Co. Based on the three sided diamonds between the hobnails, this bell may have been made by Westmoreland in the 1930s. The bell without a handle can be found as a string holder. The author believes the bell shape was made to be used both ways, as many bells are found with the same handle.

References

Anthony, Dorothy Malone. "Bell Markings and Identification." *The Bell Tower Supplement* (June-July 1971): S1-S9.

Brenner, Robert. *Depression Glass for Collectors*. Atglen, Pennsylvania: Schiffer Publishing Ltd., 1998.

Collins, Louise. "Glass Bells of the U. S. A." *The Bell Tower Supplement* (April 1976): S1-S15.

Finley, Charlie. "Glass Bells." *Glass Collector's Digest* V, no. 4 (December/January 1992): 43-46.

Florence, Gene. *Elegant Glassware of the Depression Era*. Paducah, Kentucky: Collector Books, 1993.

Hammond, Lenore and Curtis. "Collectible Glass and Porcelain Bells." *The Bell Tower Supplement* (April, 1972): S1-S27.

Heacock, William. *Fenton Glass: The Third Twenty-five Years*. Marietta, Ohio: The Glass Press, Inc., 1989 and 1994.

Kovar, Lorraine. *Westmoreland Glass, 1950-1984, Volume II*. Marietta, Ohio: Antique Publications, 1991.

Long, Milbra. "Fostoria Bells." *Glass Collector's Digest* III, no. 6 (April/May 1990): 15-17.

Long, Milbra and Emily Seate. *Fostoria, Useful and Ornamental*. Paducah, Kentucky: Collector Books, 2000.

Measell, James, ed. *Fenton Glass: The 1980s Decade*. Marietta, Ohio: The Glass Press, Inc., 1996.

Nemecek, Sylvia. "Fenton Bells." *The Bell Tower Supplement* 53, no. 6 (November-December 1995): S1-S16.

Trinidad, Jo and Al. "1893 Columbian Exposition Libbey Glass Bells." *The Bell Tower* 44, no. 6 (June-July 1986): 10.

Trinidad, Jo and Al. "Smocking Glass Bells." *The Bell Tower* 44, no. 6 (June-July 1986): 8.

Trinidad, A. A. Jr. "1893 Columbian Exposition Glass Bells Update." *The Bell Tower* 50, no. 2 (March-April 1992): 18-20.

_____. "American Glass Bells." *The Bell Tower* 50, no. 3 (May-June 1992): 14.

_____. "Mount Washington Glass Bells." *The Bell Tower* 51, no. 2 (March-April 1993): 10.

_____. "Fenton Daisy and Button Glass Bells." *The Bell Tower* 51, no. 6 (November-December 1993): 13.

_____. "Carnival Glass Bells." *The Bell Tower* 52, no. 2 (March-April 1994): 18, 19.

_____. "Imperial Slag Glass Bells." *The Bell Tower* 52, no. 5 (September-October 1994): 13.

_____. "Wide Band Glass Bells." *The Bell Tower* 53, no. 4 (July-August 1995): 10, 11.

_____. "Steuben Glass Bells." *The Bell Tower* 54, no. 2 (March-April 1996): 14.

_____. "Chocolate Glass Bells." *The Bell Tower* 54, no. 6 (November-December 1996): 24.

_____. "Victorian Belle Glass Bells." *The Bell Tower* 55, no. 2 (March-April 1997): 11.

_____. "Central Glass Works Bells." *The Bell Tower* 57, no. 2 (March-April 1999): 33.

_____. "Bells by Glen Jones." *The Bell Tower* 58, no. 1 (January-February 2000): 15, 16

_____. "Libbey Bells from the Columbian Exposition." *Glass Collector's Digest* IX, no. 4 (December/January 1996): 22-26.

Chapter Six
Glass Bells of Canada

Demaine Glass Studio
Mactaquac, New Brunswick, 1970-1980

Martin Demaine started producing glass items in 1970 in Little Bartibog, New Brunswick, under the name of Little Bartibog Glassworks. He moved to Mactaquac in 1975 and started the Demaine Glass Studio. There he began to make some glass bells. Glass articles he produced reflected the artistic expression of the Art Nouveau period. The studio was one of the largest handblown art glass studios in Canada.

All Demaine bells are unique and distinct in form and decoration. Some match sets of goblets that he made. Over a six year period he made about sixty bells.

Two Martin Demaine art glass bells. The bell on the left is clear with yellow striping and knob handle, signed Demaine 77 on outside rim. 3"d. x 5-1/2"h. $35-50. The bell on the right is mottled green/amber glass, signed Demaine Studio 78 on outside rim. 3"d. x 8-3/4"h. $75-90.

Chapter Seven

Glass Bells of England

Hodgetts, Richardson & Son
Wordsley, Stourbridge, 1870-1881

For a hundred years the name of Richardson was famous in England for producing glassware in innovative styles and techniques. During the period that W. J. Hodgetts was a principal of the firm, Hodgetts invented a threading machine (patented May 6, 1876) which permitted the application of a glass thread in a relatively uniform spacing. The bell attributed to this firm, produced about 1880, made use of this machine.

A Hodgetts, Richardson & Son blue green, blown bell with red threading on a ruffled rim. Clear hexagon pattern cut handle, clear two knop clapper. 4"d. x 6-3/4"h., c. 1880. $300-350.

John Walsh Walsh
Birmingham, 1850-1951

From 1926 to 1951, the John Walsh Walsh company produced cut glass bells with air twist handles and glass clappers. The design for the bells and glass clappers was protected under the registered design 722227, dated July 1, 1926. In the Birmingham Museum and Art Gallery there are factory records with drawings illustrating eight different cut glass patterns on bells made 7 1/2", 8 1/2", and 10 1/2" in height. Bells were sometimes marked Walsh.

Royal Brierley Crystal, Ltd.
Brierley Hill, West Midlands, 1776-

Cut glass bells having a "Royal Brierley" label have been made since the 1980s. Bells are known in Fuchsia, Jasmine, Henley, and Berkeley patterns. The company is a successor to Stevens & Williams.

Royal Brierley Crystal bells, in "Berkeley," "Fuchsia," and "Henley" patterns. 2-1/2"d. x 4-3/4"h., c. 1993. $45-60 ea.

Royal Doulton Crystal
Stourbridge, West Midlands, 1969-

Since the early twentieth century, glass products were made at the Webb Corbett factory in Stourbridge. In 1969, Webb Corbett became a part of Royal Doulton, providing elegant crystal to complement their china. Some of the cut glass bells from the 1980s have a Webb Corbett paper label. Cut glass bells produced since 1986 have a Royal Doulton paper label.

Two Royal Doulton Crystal bells. Left: a "Diamond" pattern. 2-1/4"d. x 5-1/4"h., c. 1993. $30-40. Right: a small bell by Webb-Corbett for Royal Doulton. 1-1/2"d. x 3-1/4"h., c. 1984. $20-25.

A Royal Doulton Crystal bell made for the twenty-fifth anniversary of Queen Elizabeth's Coronation, 1953-1978. Signed Bryn Smart #207 on shoulder and a crown mark above the rim. Threaded red and blue ribbon in clear handle. 3-3/4"d. x 7-3/4"h. $100-125.

Stuart & Sons, Ltd.
Wordsley, Stourbridge, 1881-

Stuart cut glass bells have been made since the 1980s. Recently, bells have been cut for them in Hungary. Stuart is a division of the Waterford Wedgwood Group.

Stuart and Sons crystal bells. On the left, a cut glass bell with one knop handle. 2-3/4"d. x 6"h., c. 1986. $50-60. On the right, a bell cut in Hungary for the millennium, in a "Cascade" pattern, 1999. 3-1/2"d. x 6-3/4"h. $50-60.

Thomas Webb & Sons
Stourbridge, 1837-1990

Thomas Webb was one of the best known glass houses in England due to their production of many high quality glass items for over 150 years, including cut and engraved glass, rock crystal glass, Burmese glass, colored glass, and cameo glass. The cut glass bells shown here were produced after the 1960s. See Chapter Eighteen for the company's Burmese bells.

Thomas Webb & Sons bells. Left to right: cut glass bell, signed Thomas Webb Crystal, 3"d. x 5-3/4"h., c. 1986. $40-50; signed Thomas Webb Crystal, 3-1/2"d. x 7-1/2"h., c. 1986. $45-55; etched with a rose and inscription to commemorate the 80th birthday of Queen Mother Elizabeth, 3-1/2"d. x 6-1/4"h., 1980. $40-50; engraved with an angel and "Christmas 1974", air twist handle, #16, signed T. Simms. 3-1/4"d. x 6-1/2"h. $200-225.

Tudor Crystal
Wordsley, Stourbridge, 1972-

Tudor Crystal has produced some cut glass bells commemorating historic events.

A Tudor Crystal bell etched with a commemoration of five hundred years since the landing of Columbus in America. 3"d. x 6-1/4"h. $60-70.

Wedgwood Glass
King's Lynn, Norfolk, 1969-1980s

The Wedgwood Group acquired King's Lynn Glass in 1969 and this division of Josiah Wedgwood & Sons, Ltd. became known as Wedgwood Glass. Special glass collections, including glass bells, have been produced at their factory near the royal residence at Sandringham to celebrate royal occasions. Most of these bells have etched designs.

Bells in blue glass, amethyst glass, and amber glass with colorless handles and Jasper medallions have been produced to celebrate various occasions and events.

Three Wedgwood clear blue glass bells with white on blue Jasper medallions. The left hand bell has a medallion showing cupid with a bow and arrow. 3-1/4"d. x 6-1/4"h. $100-120. The center bell has a horse medallion; this bell is also known in amber glass and with a white on black Jasper medallion. 3-1/4"d. x 6-1/4"h., $100-120. The right hand bell has a medallion with an Olympic torch bearer; it was issued for the 1976 Montreal Olympics. 3"d. x 5-3/4"h. $80-100.

Two Wedgwood glass bells with Jasper medallions. The bell on the left is amethyst glass with a white on Portland Blue medallion of George Washington; 750 were issued in 1976 for the American Bicentennial. 3"d. x 6"h. $60-80. The bell on the right is light blue glass with a white on blue Jasper medallion of the Liberty Bell; 1,000 were issued in 1976, also for the American Bicentennial. 2-3/4"d. x 5-3/4"h.. $70-90.

Reference

Reynolds, Eric. *The Glass of John Walsh Walsh 1850 - 1951*. Somerset, England: Richard Dennis, 1999.

Two Wedgwood glass bells with Jasper medallions of Queen Elizabeth II. The bell on the left is dark blue glass with a white on Royal Blue Jasper medallion made to celebrate the queen's silver jubilee in 1977. It has a crown and ERII on the flat top of handle, #6/175. Made for Harrods Ltd., London. 3-1/4"d. x 6"h. $150-170. The bell on the right is amethyst glass with a white on lilac Jasper made to celebrate the queen's silver jubilee. 750 of these bells were made. The back has an inscription of the jubilee and a crown and ERII. 3"d. x 5-3/4"h. $60-80.

A Wedgwood Crystal Bell commemorating the royal wedding of Charles and Diana, July 1981. 3"d. x 5-1/4"h. $40-50.

A Wedgwood Crystal bell in "Galway" pattern with silver clapper. 3"d. x 5-1/2"h., c. 1980. $35-45.

Chapter Eight

Glass Bells of Scotland

Caithness Glass

Wick, 1961-

Caithness Glass was founded in 1961 in Scotland as a part of the Royal Doulton Company. When Caithness Glass started, it initially produced handmade colored glassware. In 1968 they started to produce engraved glassware, including bells.

A clear Caithness Glass bell with an etched decoration for the millennium. 2-3/4"d. x 6-1/2"h., 2000. $35-40.

This company started as the Edinburgh and Leith Glass Company in 1867. Thomas Webb & Sons acquired the company in 1921; the name was changed to Edinburgh Crystal Glass Co. in 1955. In 1964, Crown House Limited acquired Thomas Webb & Sons and Edinburgh Crystal Glass Co. In 1987, they were incorporated into the Coloroll Group; in 1990 they became an independent company operating as the Edinburgh Crystal Glass Co., Ltd. The cut glass bells produced by Edinburgh Crystal are generally found in a thistle shape with a paper label.

Edinburgh Crystal Glass Co. bells with a thistle shape. Left to right:
"Thistle" pattern signed Edinburgh Crystal, 3"d. x 5-1/2"h., 1993;
"Braemar" pattern signed Edinburgh, 3-1/4"d. x 5-1/2"h., 1986; S.D.E.
bell signed Edinburgh Crystal, 3"d. x 5-1/2"h., 1993. $60-70 ea.

Chapter Nine
Glass Bells of Ireland ───────────────

Cavan Crystal Ltd.

Dublin Road, Cavan, 1970s–

Cavan Crystal cut glass bells have been made since the 1980s. In recent years there has been a transition in ownership.

Cavan Crystal bells in cut patterns. 3-1/4"d. x 5-1/2"h. and 3-3/4"d. x 8"h., 1980s. $30-40 ea.

Dublin Crystal Glass Company
Blackrock, Dublin, 1968–

The Dublin company has produced few cut glass bells.

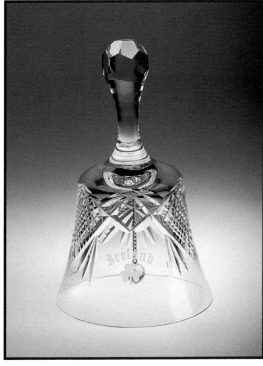

A Dublin Crystal Glass Co. cut glass bell etched with "Ireland" and a shamrock. 3-1/2"d. x 6"h., 1980s. $40-50.

A Galway Crystal bell cut in a diamond pattern with a cut ring handle. 3-1/4"d. x 6-1/4"h. $40-50.

Galway Irish Crystal, Ltd.
Dublin Road, Galway, 1967–

Galway has produced bells in three patterns, called "Leah," "Marriage," and "Claddagh"; some were made in two sizes. The "Leah" bell shown is known also with a straight handle.

Tipperary Crystal Designs, Ltd.
Ballynoran, Carrick-on-Suir,
Tipperary, 1988–

Tipperary bells are cut in a heavy crystal.

A Galway Crystal bell cut in the "Leah" pattern. 2-1/2"d. x 3-3/4"h., c. 1980s. $30-40.

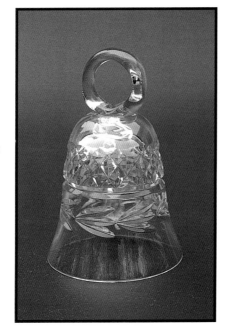

A Tipperary Crystal bell cut in a "Diamond" pattern. 2-3/4"d. x 5"h., 1990s. $50-60.

Tyrone Crystal
Killybrackey, Dungannon,
Northern Ireland, 1971-

Tyrone Crystal produces lead crystal items with a lead oxide content of over thirty percent. The company currently produces four different cut glass bells.

A pair of Tyrone Crystal "Bangor" pattern bells; the company also makes bells in "Bronagh," "Belfast," and "Abbeyfeale" patterns. 1-3/4"d. x 4"h. and 2-3/4"d. x 6"h., 1980s and 1990s. $35-55 ea.

Waterford Crystal bells. Left to right: Christmas 1988, 1-3/4"d. x 5"h.; Cunard Line 150th anniversary, 1840-1990, 3-1/2"d. x 4"h.; Bicentennial bell on base plate, bell 3-3/4"d. x 4"h.; and "Colleen" pattern bell, 3-1/4"d. x 5"h. $70-90 ea.

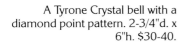

A Tyrone Crystal bell with a diamond point pattern. 2-3/4"d. x 6"h. $30-40.

Waterford Crystal bells. Left to right: pattern 125/144, 3"d. x 4-3/4"h., c. 1976; pattern 125/145, 2-3/4"d. x 4-1/2"h., c. 1986; "Lismore" pattern, 3"d. x 5-1/4"h., c. 1990; "Lismore" pattern, 2-1/2"d. x 4-3/4"h., c. 1990. $60-80 ea.

Waterford Crystal Ltd.
Kilbarry, Waterford, 1947 -

Waterford Crystal has produced many cut glass bells since its formation in 1947. By the 1980s, Waterford Crystal was the largest producer of hand-crafted crystal in the world. Many of the patterns on bells match those of various tableware items. Bells are produced also in an annual series and to commemorate special events. The bells are cut in a heavy crystal. Some bells made under the Marquis name have been made in mainland Europe for Waterford.

A Waterford Marquis Millennium bell cut with a trailing star and 2000. Made in Germany. 2-1/2"d. x 4-1/4"h. $30-40.

Chapter Ten

Glass Bells of Austria ——————————

Several Austrian firms have produced glass bells, but the best known is Swarovski & Company. Bells from other Austrian companies are difficult to distinguish from those of nearby countries.

A glass bell with a crystal swan handle similar to Swarovski glass but of unknown maker. 3-1/4"d. x 5-1/4"h., c. 1996. $80-100.

Two Austrian cut glass bells of unknown maker. 2-1/4"d. x 4-1/2"h., c. 1986. $25-30.

Swarovski & Company
Wattens, 1895-

Swarovski has produced four bells since it began producing novelty items in the 1970s. The company is well known for its sparkling cut glass containing more than thirty percent lead oxide.

Swarovski glass bells. Shown are three sizes of bells with floral decorations, 2-3/4"d. x 5-1/2"h., 2"d. x 4-1/2"h., and 1-1/2"d. x 3-1/4"h. $45-125 ea.; a "Solaris" pattern bell with cut loop handle and colored cabochons, 2"d. x 4-1/2"h., 1999. $100-135; and a bell shaped miniature, 1"h. $35-45.

Chapter Eleven

Glass Bells of Belgium

Val St. Lambert
Liège, 1825–

A Val St. Lambert catalog from 1939 shows line drawings of many cut glass bells. It is not known if all these bells were produced, but many of them can be found. Other bells appeared in catalogs from 1940 through 1977.

Three Val St. Lambert bells in clear engraved glass, c. 1939. Pattern numbers refer to a 1939/1940 catalog. Left to right: #758/60B, 2-3/4"d x 5-1/2"h.; #128/39, 2-1/4"d. x 4-1/4"h.; #105/39, 2-3/4"d. x 5-1/2"h. $30-40 ea.

Two Val St. Lambert bells, one light green glass with clear handle, the other in clear glass with some light etching. 2-3/4"d. x 4-3/4"h., c. 1939. $35-45 ea.

Three Val St. Lambert bells in clear engraved glass. Left to right: a 1950 bell made for the "Around the World Shoppers Club." 2-1/2"d. x 4-1/2"h. $40-50; a bell with an engraved tic-tac-toe pattern. 2-1/4"d. x 4-1/4"h., c. 1939. $20-30; a bell with a cross diamond pattern. 2-1/4"d. x 4-1/4"h., c. 1939. $20-30.

Two similar Val St. Lambert bells in clear engraved glass, #112/39 "Suzanne" pattern. 2-1/2"d. x 5"h., c. 1939. $25-35 ea.

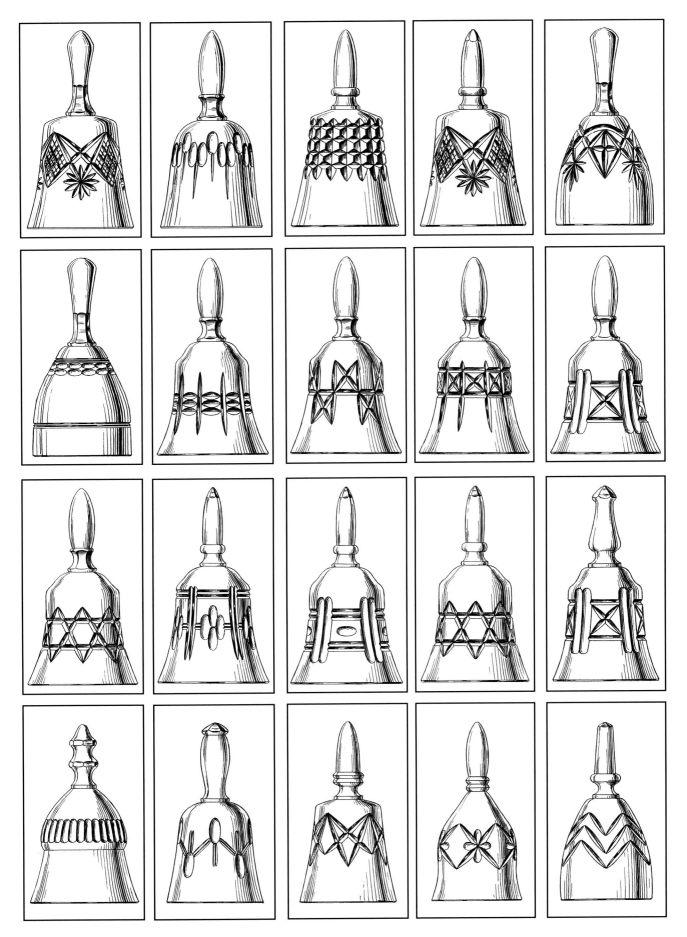

These line drawings were part of the 1939 Val St. Lambert catalog of bells. *Courtesy of Val Saint Lambert, Belgium.*

Reference

Trinidad, A. A. Jr. "Val St. Lambert Bells." *The Bell Tower* 51, No. 4 (July-August 1993): 14-18.

Chapter Twelve
Glass Bells of Bohemia

Bohemian glass is a general term used for glass made in parts of Czechoslovakia (now the Czech Republic and Slovakia), Austria, Germany, and Poland. Bells are found to have Bohemian glass labels without identifying the manufacturer. They exist in three main types of glass: flashed glass, cut cased glass, and cut clear glass. The flashed and cased glass bells have patterns engraved or cut through the outer layer of glass to reveal the colored glass below. Many cased glass bells also have painted decoration applied. The Bohemian cut clear glass bells are more recent. Bells are known to have been made by Egermann, Moser, and Sklo glass companies.

Two Bohemian ruby faceted glass bells, c. 1850. The bell on the left has a bronze coiled serpent handle and is 2-3/4"d. x 5-3/4"h. The bell on the right has a bronze leaf handle and is 3"d. x 5-3/4"h. $200-250 ea.

Bohemian glass bells attributed to Moser, c. 1950s. The three smaller bells are in blue, cranberry, and green flashed glass on eight panels surrounded by gold decoration. 2-3/4"d. x 5"h. $60-80 ea. The taller bell has blue panels and is 3-1/4"d. x 6"h. $150-175.

Bohemian bells in engraved flashed glass, 1970s-1980s: a pheasant on amber glass with painted gold decoration, clear handle, 3"d. x 5-1/2"h.; a pheasant on red glass with painted decoration, clear handle, 3-1/4"d. x 5-1/2"h.; a deer and trees on red glass with amber handle, 3"d. x 5-3/4"h.; and a butterfly on red glass with amber handle, 3-1/4"d. x 5-1/2"h. $40-60 ea.

Four Bohemian bells in engraved flashed glass: red, blue, and amber bells with deer and tower scene; and a red bell with bird and castle scene. 3-1/4"d. x 5-1/2"h., 1970s-1980s. $40-55 ea.

Three Bohemian bells in engraved flashed red glass with vintage and floral scenes. 3"d. x 5-1/4"h., 1980s-1990s. $30-40 ea.

Four Bohemian bells from the Czech Republic in cased white glass, cut to reveal the green or pink glass below, painted with floral decoration, clear handles. 3-1/4"d. x 5-1/2"h., 1980s-1990s. $50-80 ea.

Bohemian flashed glass bells with gold decoration, 1990s. Left to right: cranberry, 3-1/4"d. x 6-3/4"h.; blue, 3-1/2"d. x 6"h.; cranberry, 3-1/2"d. x 6-1/4"h. $30-40 ea.

Four Bohemian bells in cased white glass, cut to reveal the blue, pink, or green glass below, painted with floral decoration, clear handles. 2-3/4"d. x 5"h., 1980s. $45-75 ea.

Three Bohemian bells with gold overlay of colored glass, painted and applied flowers, 1980s-1990s. The two in the front are green glass, 2-3/4"d. x 4-1/4"h., $20-25 ea.; the rear bell is amber glass, 3-1/4"d. x 5-1/2"h., $40-50.

A Czech Republic art glass bell painted in red, green, and yellow. 2-3/4"d. x 5-3/4"h. $40-50.

A Bohemian bell in amber to red glass with a clear handle. 3-1/4"d. x 5-1/2"h., 1980s. $50-60.

Bohemian bells painted in white with children in the Mary Gregory style. Sizes vary from 3"d. x 4-3/4"h. to 3"d. x 5-3/4"h., 1970-1990s. $35-50 ea.

Top left: Bohemian cut glass bells with similar designs. 2-3/4"d. x 5"h., 1990s. $25-35 ea.

Bottom left: Two Bohemian bells with the same design of two rows of cut hobstars. The bell on the left was made by the Sklo Glass Co., Zvonek in 1999 and is 2-3/4"d. x 5-1/2"h. The bell on the right is 2-1/2"d. x 5"h., 1990s. $20-30 ea.

Top right: A very heavy, cut glass bell from Czechoslovakia cut with three rows of hobstars. 4-3/4"d. x 9-1/2"h., 1980s. $80-90.

Bottom right: Bohemian cut glass bells of various shapes and designs. 2-3/4"d x 5"h., 1990s. $30-50 ea.

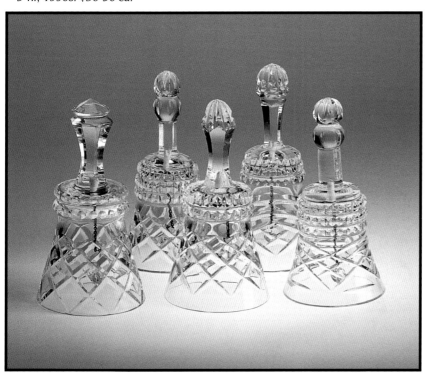

Top left: Two similar heavy cut glass bells, probably Bohemian. 4"d. x 6"h. and 3-1/4"d. x 5-1/4"h. $50-60 ea.

Top right: Two cut glass bells of similar crosscut diamond and fan design, probably Bohemian. Unusual seven sided handle. 2-1/4"d. x 3-1/4"h. and 2-1/2"d. x 4-1/2"h. $25-35 ea.

Center: A clear glass bell with swirls of bubbles, etched with "Czechoslova-kia" along the rim, hexagonal handle. 2-1/4"d. x 4"h., $20-30.

Bottom right: A clear green glass bell with gold decoration, probably late nineteenth century Bohemian. Brass clapper on chain attached to twisted wire embedded in the handle. 3-1/4"d. x 6-1/4"h. $125-150.

Chapter Thirteen

Glass Bells of France

There are many fine bells produced by several well known glass companies in France. Any "wedding bells" attributed to a French company are shown in Chapter Eighteen. Some glass bells of clear, translucent, or opaline glass with gold decoration and with a short, solid, round handle are known to bell collectors as being of French origin, but the maker is not known to the author.

Compagnie des Cristalleries de Baccarat Lorraine, 1823–

Baccarat has been one of the most important makers of crystal glass in France. In the 1850s, the company introduced colored glassware and this is probably the time period when glass bells known as French flint glass bells were made by Baccarat. The European Bell Institute, L'Isle-Jourdan, France, believes the original idea for these bells came from Bayreuth in Bavaria, where they were made in the late eighteenth century.

The bells in clear glass with a multifaceted top of handle were designed by Baccarat in 1956 and made in two sizes. The larger of two known bells has the etched Baccarat seal at the base of the handle.

Two Baccarat crystal bells with multi-faceted handles and teardrop clappers, first produced in the 1950s. 2-3/4"d. x 5-1/4"h. and 3-1/2"d. x 6-1/2"h. $100-140 ea.

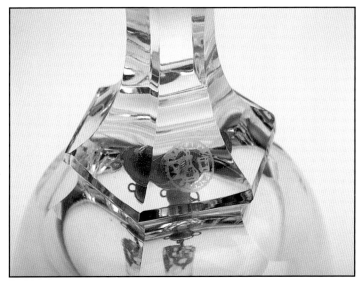

Etched Baccarat seal at base of handle on the Baccarat bells.

The following table shows the various combinations of handles and coordinated clappers on French flint glass bells known by the author. Several bells are known with "baccarat" inscribed; more are seen with "France" inscribed. Many bells are known with a ball clapper and are not listed unless the handle with a coordinated clapper is not known by the author. The handles are believed to be made of decorated Vienna bronze.

French Flint Glass Bells

Handle	Clapper	Color				
		Green	Blue	Amyth.	Red	Amber
Antelope	Acorn	x				
Bear on four legs	Fish	x		x		
Bear on four legs	Honeycomb	x				
Bear on hind legs	Loaf of bread	x				
Bird	Wafer	x				
Bird	Berries			x		
Black boy	Banjo	x				
Black boy	Orange	x				
Cat	Mouse	x		x		x
Crab & shell	Shrimp	x				
Deer	Pine cone	x				
Devil	Green bead	x				
Devil	Pitchfork	x				
Elephant	Honeycomb	x				
French poodle	Bone	x		x		
French poodle on four legs	Bone	x				
Goat	Acorn	x				
Lion	Bone	x				
Monkey	Pineapple	x				
Ostrich	Egg	x		x		
Owl	Skull	x	x			
Pheasant	Berry	x				
Pheasant	Pine cone	x				
Rabbit	Carrot	x				
Rooster	Egg on leg	x		x		
Rooster	Egg on leg			x*		
Skeleton	Skull	x				
Swan	Ball				x	
Wild boar	Acorn	x		x		

The glass of all bells has a square shape except where noted by an asterisk (*). That bell has a conical shape in cut glass.

A French flint glass bell with a rooster handle and clapper of an egg on a leg. The glass is cut pale amethyst, of unusual design for these bells with coordinated handles and clappers. 2-1/2"d. x 4-1/2"h., nineteenth century. $900-1,100.

Egg on a leg clapper for bell with rooster handle.

Green flint glass bell with copper leaf handle and hollow metal clapper on stiff wire. This bell exists in amethyst glass also. 3"d. x 4-1/2"h. $200-250.

A pair of French flint glass bells with French poodles as handles and bones as clappers, in green and amethyst glass. 1-3/4"sq. x 4-1/4"h. $700-900 ea.

Amethyst and green French flint glass bells, nineteenth century: Cat handle and mouse clapper, 1-1/2"sq. x 4"h.; bird handle and wafer clapper, 1-1/2"sq. x 3-3/4"h.; wild boar handle with acorn clapper, 1-1/2"sq. x 4"h. $700-1,000 ea.

Cristalleries Royales de Champagne
Bayel, 1666

Bayel crystal bells are known for the frosted handles of animals and historic figures.

Two Bayel Cristallin clear glass bells with frosted animal handles: owl on the left and sea horse on the right. 3-1/4"d. x 7"h., 1980s. $20-30 ea.

Daum Frères
Nancy, 1875-1962

The Daum glassworks started in the 1870s and began producing crystal items in 1950. Bells have been produced in clear lead glass and sometimes etched to commemorate events. All are signed in script "Daum, France." In 1962, the company became Cristallerie de Nancy.

Two signed Daum, France crystal bells. Left: commemorates Pope John Paul II's visit to the United States in 1979, flame handle, 70/2500, 3-1/4"d. x 5-3/4"h. Right: variable thickness loop handle, 3-1/4"d. x 5"h. $75-90 ea.

Cristallerie Lalique et Cie
Wingen-sur-Moder, 1918-

René Lalique began his first experiments with glass in 1893 and started mass production of glass items in 1905. He acquired a glass house in its present location in 1918 and it continues to produce glass items today. Two clear glass bells with frosted swallow handles are known, one with open wings and the other with closed wings. The bells are signed "Lalique, France" in script at the base of the handle.

Two Lalique crystal bells with frosted swallow handles, teardrop clappers. One with open wings, 3-1/2"d. x 5-1/2"h.; one with closed wings, 3-3/4"d. x 5"h. Signed Lalique, France just below the birds. 1980s. $80-100 ea.

Compagnie des Cristalleries de St. Louis Lorraine, 1767–

St. Louis was the first on the European continent to perfect the manufacture of lead crystal. Bells made since World War II are usually etched with "St. Louis, France" in a circle on the top of the handle.

A St. Louis cobalt blue bell cut to clear with stars. Clear round handle with St. Louis seal on top. 2"d. x 2-3/4"h. $200-225.

French Bells of Unknown Origin

There are some bells with gold decoration which bell collectors believe are made in France, but their producer presently is unknown.

Four similar bells, all attributed to France. Left to right: pink opaline with gilded flowers, 2-1/2"d. x 4"h.; clear with gold flower decoration, 2-3/4"d. x 4"h.; translucent white with gold striping , 3"d. x 4"h.; and opaline with gold garlands and ribbons, 2-1/2"d. x 4"h. All have short, solid glass handles. $30-50 ea.

References

Peffer, Becky. "French Flint Glass Bells." *The Bell Tower Supplement* (May-June 1980): 8 pages.

Trinidad, Al. "Ask a Question - Get an Answer." *The Bell Tower* 53, no. 2 (March-April 1995): 13.

Chapter Fourteen
Glass Bells of Germany

Many glass bells were made in Germany before and after the unification of East and West Germany. The glass bells usually are labeled with their country of origin, but seldom do they show the name of the manufacturer. Many pressed/cut glass bells have been made by the House of Goebel Handelsges in Munich and they can be identified by paper labels.

Three German cut glass bells, 1980s. Left to right: amber cut to clear glass with tapered cut handle, 1-1/2"d. x 4-3/4"h.; green cut to clear glass, 2-3/4"d. x 7-1/4"h.; and amber cut to clear with cut handle, 3-1/4"d. x 7-1/4"h. $35-50 ea.

Two bells from East Germany, 1990s. Left: white overlay cut to reveal green glass below and painted with flowers and gold striping, clear handle, 3"d. x 7"h. Right: clear red glass with gold band overlay, clear handle, 3"d. x 7"h. $40-50 ea.

Two House of Goebel bells with a hexagonal button design in purple and red. 2-1/2"d. x 5-1/4"h., 1980s. $40-50 ea.

Two German bells of similar cut design,, 1950s. The smaller bell, 2-3/4"d. x 3-1/2"h., has a label with "Made in U. S. Zone of Germany." The larger bell is 3-1/2"d. x 4-1/2"h. $30-45 ea.

Label for the bell made in U. S. Zone of Germany.

A Goebel glass bell with silver filigree handle. 2-3/4"d. x 8"h., 1980s. $40-50.

A clear glass Goebel bell, in a Biedermeier style, with engraved flowers. 3"d. x 6-3/4"h., 1980s. $30-40.

A Goebel clear glass bell with ceramic little boy clapper, from their "Dolly Dingle" series. 3-1/4"d. x 6-3/4"h., c. 1980s. $30-40.

German bells engraved with quails on left, flowers on right. 2-3/4"d. x 4-3/4"h. $30-35 ea.

Center left: A variety of West German cut glass bells, from 2-1/4"d. x 3-1/2"h. to 3"d. x 6"h. 1960s-1970s. $30-45 ea.

Center right: Three West German cut glass bells. Left to right: 2-3/4"d. x 5-1/4"h., $20-30; 3-1/2"d. x 6-1/4"h., $50-60; 2-1/2"d. x 5-1/2"h., $40-50.

Bottom left: Two German bells in a hexagonal shape with scalloped rim, one in clear and one in amber to ruby glass. 4"d. x 4-1/2"h. $25-30 ea.

Bottom right: Two very heavy glass bells, 1980s. The left bell is from West Germany and is cut in pinwheels and cross-hatched squares, 4-1/2"d. x 9-1/4"h.; the right bell is from East Germany and has cross hatching in diamonds, 4-3/4"d. x 9-3/4"h. $50-60 ea.

Reference
Lange, Anselm. *Europäische Tischglocken.* Hannover: Minner-Verlag, 1981.

Two Italian millefiore bells with clown handles. Left: 3-1/4"d. x 6-1/4"h., c. 1990. $125-150. Right: frosted glass, 3-1/4"d. x 6"h., c. 1980. $40-50.

Chapter Fifteen

Glass Bells of Italy

The oldest Italian glass bells can be traced to the early seventeenth century. Since the end of World War II, many glass bells have been made in Italy with paper labels usually listing only the island of Murano as the origin.

Left to right, top to bottom: Italian millefiore bells made from colored canes. Left to right: frosted ring handle, 3"d. x 5-1/4"h., c. 1995; frosted ring handle, 4"d. x 5-1/2"h., c. 1973; clear twisted ring handle, 3-1/4"d. x 4"h., c. 1998; frosted ring handle, 3"d. x 5"h., c. 1984. $40-60 ea.

Three Italian millefiore bells with frosted animal handles, 1980s-1990s. Left to right: elephant handle, 2-3/4"d. x 5"h., $40-50; pigeon handle, 2-3/4"d. x 5"h., $15-20; and fish handle, 3"d. x 5"h., $50-60.

Italian millefiore bells, both with gold flecked handles, c. 1993. Pink, 3-1/2"d. x 5-1/2"h., $80-100; multicolor, 3-1/2"d. x 6-3/4"h., $60-80.

Three Italian bells with applied fruit or leaves, 1990s. Left to right: cased blue on white glass with applied cherries and blue teardrop clapper, 3-3/4"d. x 5-1/4"h., $50-70; Burmese type glass with applied leaves, clear teardrop clapper, 4"d. x 5"h., $60-80; cased lavender on white glass with applied grapes, three prong frosted orange handle, and frosted orange teardrop clapper, 4"d. x 5-1/4"h., $70-90.

Three Italian quilted pattern bells on cased glass, color on white, 1970s-1980s. Left to right: blue, 3-1/4"d. x 5-1/4"h.; blue, 4"d. x 5-1/2"h.; lavender, 3-1/4"d. x 5-1/4"h. $35-50 ea.

Three Italian bells using twisted glass canes, *vetro a retorti.* Left to right: green, gold, and white twisted canes, 3-1/2"d. x 4"h., 1990s; pink, yellow, and blue twisted canes, 4-1/2"d. x 5-1/4"h., 1990s; white canes, 2-3/4"d. x 4-1/2"h., 1980s. $40-50 ea.

Italian bells with swirled pattern. Left to right: white on frosted glass, 3-1/2"d. x 4-1/2"h., c. 1982; pink on clear glass, 3-3/4"d. x 4-1/4"h., c. 1995; white on clear glass with gold on clear glass twisted handle, 2-3/4"d. x 4-1/2"h., c. 1980. $30-40 ea.

Three modern Italian multicolored glass bells, 1998. Left to right: 1-3/4"d. x 4-3/4"h., 2-1/4"d. x 5"h., 1-3/4"d. x 3-3/4"h. $50-60 ea.

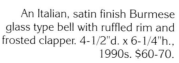

Two Italian flashed glass bells with Coca Cola advertising. 3-1/4"d. x 5-1/4"h. and 2-3/4"d. x 5-1/4"h., 1970s-1980s. $40-45 ea.

An Italian translucent pearl glass bell with blue handle and scalloped rim. 4"d. x 6"h., c. 1980s. $120-140.

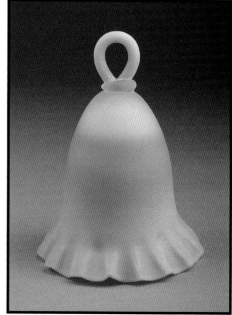

An Italian, satin finish Burmese glass type bell with ruffled rim and frosted clapper. 4-1/2"d. x 6-1/4"h., 1990s. $60-70.

Chapter Sixteen
Other European Glass Bells ————————

There are glass companies in some European countries that are known to have produced only a few glass bells. Towards the end of the twentieth century, however, many bells were being made in eastern European countries, particularly Hungary, Poland, Romania, and Yugoslavia.

Norway

The Hadelands Glasverk at Jevnaker, Oppland, has produced crystal and colored glass items since the 1850s. A glass bell from the 1980s is made of very hard brittle glass. The Magnor Glassverk has produced clear glass bells with applied flowers and fruit.

Left: a Norwegian clear glass bell with two knop handle and painted berries made by Magnor Glassverk. 3-1/4"d. x 6-1/2"h., c. 1994. $80-90. Right: a swirled brittle glass bell made by Hadeland. 3-3/4"d. x 3-1/2"h., c. 1983. $20-30.

Poland

Since the 1980s, some Polish glass companies have produced bells in clear and colored cut and engraved glass. Some of the bells have used a flashed glass.

A deep ruby cased glass bell from Poland cut with floral motif to clear glass, with cut clear glass handle. 3-1/4"d. x 6"h., c. 1978. $30-40.

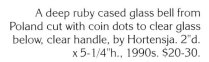

A deep ruby cased glass bell from Poland cut with coin dots to clear glass below, clear handle, by Hortensja. 2"d. x 5-1/4"h., 1990s. $20-30.

Portugal

Since the 1960s, clear colored glass bells with air twist handles have been produced in Portugal, with labels marked Violetta.

A clear glass bell from Portugal with a cut pattern and air twist handle. This bell is also found in several colors. 3"d. x 6-1/4"h., c. 1960s. $20-30.

Sweden

Two Swedish companies are noted for their production of glass bells: Kosta Boda and Orrefors.

A clear glass bell from Kosta Boda, Sweden, cut with flowers in a design by Monica Backström. 3"d. x 5-3/4"h. $40-50.

Russia

In recent years glass bells with cut designs have been made in the city of Gus Khrustalniy.

This clear glass bell with brass orthodox cross and cut star pattern is from Gus Khrustalniy, Russia. 2"d. x 5-3/4"h., c. 1998. $30-40.

A pair of bells by Paracin, in Yugoslavia. Clear glass with gold bands on the shoulder and at the bottom of the base, flowers cut through the flashed amber or blue glass above. 3-1/4"d. x 5-1/2"h., c. 1992. $20-30 ea.

Yugoslavia

Bells made by Paracin are of clear glass with bands of color and engraved flowers and leaves. Newer glass bells are usually clear glass with etching or engraving.

Chapter Seventeen

Glass Bells of Venezuela ———————————

ICET *Art Murano*

Potrerito

Some glass workers from Murano migrated to Venezuela in the 1950s and, in more recent years, formed ICET Art Murano to produce art glass articles — including several free blown bells.

A milk white glass with multicolored areas in a Murano type glass from the ICET Art Murano company in Potrerito, Venezuela. 3-1/4"d. x 4-1/4"h. $50-60.

Chapter Eighteen
Wedding Bells

A milk white bell with ruby rim and a clear green glass handle with one green knop and one white knop. 4-3/4"d. x 11-1/2"h. $425-475.

General Information

A wedding bell is a term that has been used generally by bell collectors for relatively large blown glass bells, primarily of English origin, made in two parts and joined together by plaster of paris. From the mid-eighteenth century to the early twentieth century, the period during which most of them were made, these bells were given sometimes as wedding presents. Sometimes a pair, known as lady and gentleman bells, was given. Clappers were usually of the glass teardrop variety, in clear glass or various colors, attached to a stiff, U-shaped wire embedded in the plaster. Because most clappers were attached loosely, many bells today have no clappers or have replacements. The top of the handles usually end with a finial of one to seven graduated balls or layers of glass known as knops. The knops are sometimes colored to match or complement the color of the bell.

Below, left to right:
A red bell with a three knop clear blue handle. 5"d. x 11-1/4"h. $300-350.

A red bell with a blue handle and five red knops. 4-3/4"d. x 10-3/4"h. $450-500.

A cranberry glass bell with a three knop clear green glass handle. 5-3/4"d. x 13"h. $300-350.

A light amethyst swirled glass bell with a three knop clear, light blue handle. 5"d. x 9-1/2"h. $275-325.

English Wedding Bells

In 1745, an excise tax was imposed in England that was based on the weight of the glass and the weight of its ingredients. This tax was increased gradually, so that light, blown glass articles were popular, while heavier, lead glass articles could be afforded only by the affluent. Because of this tax, the output of glass bells was greatest between 1820 and 1850, when the demand for light weight, blown colored glass was at its peak. Many of the bells were produced by glass blowers in companies that made window glass and bottles. The tax was repealed in 1845 and some heavier glass bells were made thereafter. The bells gradually were produced commercially by glass houses in England through the end of the nineteenth century.

The earlier bells were known as friggers, or whimsies, because they were thought to have been produced by glass workers on their own time. A Newcastle, England newspaper in 1830 reported a procession of the Guild of Glassmakers carrying their wares through the streets of the city. It said "Some carried a glass bell which they rang lustily." Can anyone imagine ringing a glass bell lustily?

The earliest English wedding bells were made between 1750 and 1850. Although two English towns are associated with these bells, they are known primarily for the window glass and colored glass bottles they produced. The town of Nailsea had the Nailsea Glassworks for eighty-five years from 1788 to 1873, and nearby Bristol had about fifteen glass houses, primarily between 1750 and 1850.

A characteristic of Nailsea bells is latticinio type loops, colored or white, distributed on clear or colored glass in a wavy, festooned, feathery, or zigzag pattern. Today, any glass with these loops is known as Nailsea type glass.

A clear glass bell with red Nailsea loops and mechanical red threading; the handle has two small knops. 4-1/2"d. x 10-1/2"h. $400-450.

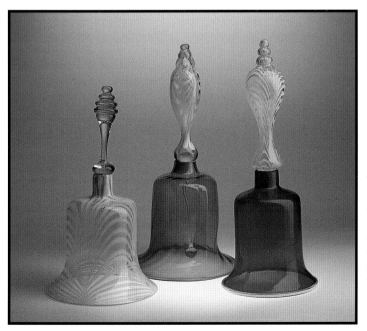

Three bells with white loops typical of Nailsea type bells. Left to right: a clear glass bell with white loops and a four knop handle, 6-1/4"d. x 10-3/4"h.; a cranberry glass bell with a white rim and a three knop hollow handle with white loops, 6-1/2"d. x 13"h.; a red glass bell with a white rim and a three knop hollow handle with white loops, 5-1/4"d. x 13-1/4"h. $250-300 ea.

Bristol glass houses produced articles in many colors, but their most famous was Bristol Blue, a dark clear royal blue which was popular in the second half of the eighteenth century. They were also known for a ruby red and an opaque white glass. Bells with a diamond quilted pattern, made around 1880, are associated with Bristol.

Green was not a popular color and fewer bells are seen in that color. The rarer colors for wedding bells are believed to be yellow, orange, and purple. The most common colors are red and cranberry.

Left: A bell in Bristol blue glass with three knop clear glass handle. 5-1/2"d. x 11"h. $250-300.

Right: A clear green bell with three knop clear handle. 5-1/4"d. x 12-1/4"h. $200-250.

An orange glass bell with a clear handle and a complex knop finial. 5"d. x 10-3/4"h. $300-375.

Left: A yellow bell with blue rim and a clear wrythen molded three knop handle. 5"d. x 9-1/2"h. $225-275.

Right: An opaline to clear glass bell with a three knop clear glass handle. 5"d. x 10-3/4"h. $250-300.

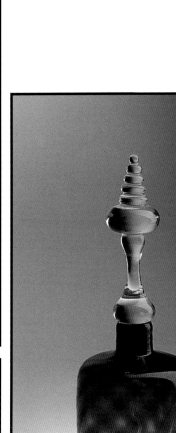

Left: A red bell with a raised rim and a sharply pointed clear glass handle. 4-1/2"d. x 10"h. $275-325.

Right: A red bell with a clear handle. The handle has three cobalt blue knops and one clear knop. 4-3/4"d. x 10-1/2"h. $250-300.

An amethyst swirled glass bell with a five knop clear glass handle. Possibly from the eighteenth century because of the short handle. 5-1/4"d. x 11"h. $250-300.

Left: A red bell with a five knop clear glass handle and a blue teardrop clapper, 8-1/2"d. 15-3/4"h. $350-400.

Right: A red bell with a four knop lime green clear glass handle. 6-1/4"d. x 13"h. $300-350.

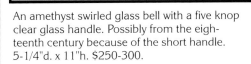

Handles generally have an inverted balustrade shape and are mostly found in a clear glass, often colored. Some bells and handles have a twisted ribbing pattern, known in England as a wrythen pattern. Often a thin thread of glass is applied to the outer surface in a random or regular pattern known as threading. On some bells, this threading has been added to the partially blown base glass and the glass has then been rolled on a metal bed before being fully blown to produce a smooth surface. On English glass with uniformly spaced threading produced by machine, the spacing of threads is usually between 20 and 22 threads per inch.

A green bell with white threading and a clear twisted glass handle with wrythen ribbing and three knops. 5-1/2"d. x 11-3/4"h. $350-400.

A clear bright blue bell with a five knop clear wrythen handle. 5-1/4"d. x 9-1/2"h. $225-275.

A cranberry glass bell with a swirled pattern and a white rim. The wrythen handle has four knops. 5-1/2"d. x 12-1/2"h. c. 1820. $300-350.

A clear green bell with white random striping along the rim and a three knop clear glass handle with green swirls. 4-1/2"d. x 10-1/4"h. c. 1850s. $300-325.

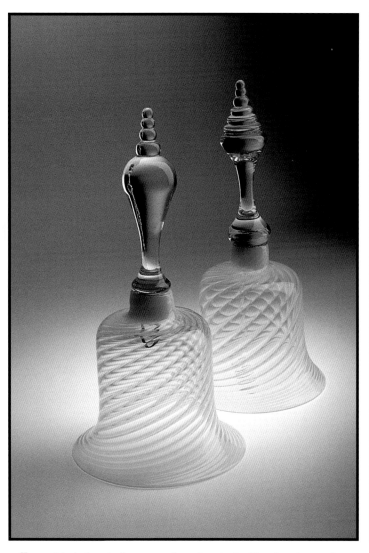

Two swirled glass bells: an opaline glass bell with a four knop clear glass handle, 4-3/4"d. x 9-1/4"h., and a blue opaline glass bell with a six knop clear inverted balustrade handle, 4-1/2"d. x 9-3/4"h. $275-325 ea.

Two bells with threading that was applied when the bell was partially blown and then fully blown to incorporate the threading in a smooth glass finish. Left: a clear glass bell with white threading and a three knop clear glass handle, 5-1/2"d. x 12-1/2"h. Right: a clear glass bell with red threading and a white handle with three blue knops, possibly made for a patriotic event, 4-1/4"d. x 10"h. $250-300 ea.

Three bells with random white threading, c. 1850s. Left to right: lemon colored bell with a three knop clear glass handle encasing a lemon striping, 5"d. x 10"h.; brown bell with a three knop clear glass handle encasing a brown and white threading, 5"d. x 11"h.; green bell with a clear glass handle with two clear knops and one green knop, 5"d. x 11-3/4"d. $325-375 ea.

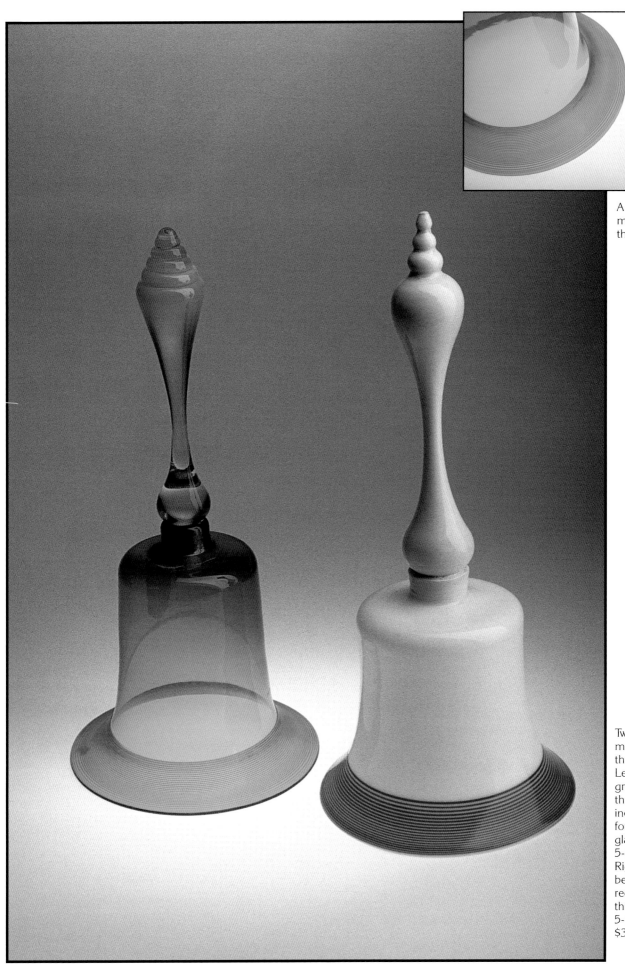

A close-up of the mechanical threading.

Two bells with machine applied threading, c. 1890s. Left: a clear, blue green bell with white threading along one inch of rim, and a four knop vaseline glass handle, 5-1/2"d. x 11-1/2"h. Right: a milk glass bell with one inch of red threading and three knop handle, 5-1/4"d. x 12"h. $375-425 ea.

Bells are found with red, white, and blue colors thought to have been produced to celebrate patriotic events. Some bells have the three colors as a glass ribbon embedded in a clear glass handle. These may have been produced for the Great Exhibition of 1851 in the Crystal Palace in London, considered to be the first World's Fair.

Two bells with twisted red, white, and blue ribbon in a two knop clear glass handle. The left bell is ruby glass with thin white rim, 4-1/2"d. x 10-3/4"h. The right bell is white with a red rim, 4-3/4"d. x 10-1/2"h. Both may have been made for the 1851 Great Exhibition in the Crystal Palace, London, considered to be the first World's Fair. $475-525 ea.

In 1885, the Mount Washington Glass Company of New Bedford, Massachusetts patented a pink to yellow colored glass known as Burmese. The glass was licensed to be produced in England by Thomas Webb and Sons, a well known firm in Stourbridge. Burmese glass bells produced by Webb are found with clear green or colorless glass handles in several sizes.

Large wedding bells are believed to have been produced late in the Victorian era. Towards the end of the nineteenth century, some bells were made having a diameter of up to 18" at the base. The bells of that era usually have many knops and their shape is sometimes exaggerated. During this same period, the handle or the finial of the handle was sometimes made into a hand, foot, bird, or flowers.

A swirled cranberry glass bell with a three knop clear handle. 6-1/4"d. x 14-1/4"h. $275-325.

A red bell with white rim, clear glass handle with three custard glass and three clear glass knops. 6-1/4"d. x 12-1/2"h. $300-350.

A cranberry glass bell with a clear handle and five clear amber knops. 6-3/4" x 15-1/4"h. $350-400.

A light amethyst swirled glass bell with opal rim, light blue clear glass handle with four knops. 7-1/4"d. x 16"h. $350-400.

A milk white bell with a translucent green glass handle in the shape of a hand. 4-3/4"d. x 10"h., c. 1880s. $450-500.

Opposite page

Four Burmese glass bells with clear green handles made by Thomas Webb & Sons, licensed in 1896 by the Mount Washington Glass Co. of New Bedford, Massachusetts to produce Burmese glass articles in England. Back row: three knop green handle, 3"d. x 7-1/4"h. $200-250; two knop green handle with twisted ribbing known as wrythen, 5"d. x 11"h. $500-600. Front row: three knop green handle, 2-1/2"d. x 6-1/2"h. $175-225; green handle, 2-1/2"d. x 4-3/4"h. $150-200.

Smaller wedding bells, under 10" in height with the handle less in height than the body of the bell, are believed to be the oldest, from the second half of the eighteenth century. The handles of these bells have a clear grayish cast.

Some writers on English glass state that cut glass handles on wedding bells first appeared in 1783 and associate cut glass handles with the eighteenth century.

A blue wedding type bell in a swirled pattern with a clear glass handle and four knops, the top one being gray. The handle is less than half the total height of the bell, an indication that it may be from the eighteenth century. 5-1/2"d. x 10-1/2"h. $250-300.

A bright blue bell with a milk glass handle and three blue knops. 3-1/2"d. x 7-1/4"h. $300-350.

A small white bell with green rim and clear glass handle. 3"d. x 6"h. $150-200.

A cranberry glass bell with raised rim and clear, seven-sided cut glass handle with serrated corners. The first cut glass handles on wedding bells were made in the late eighteenth century. 5-1/4"d. x 11-3/4"h. $300-400.

About thirty years ago, some English wedding bells were exhibited at a gallery in New York City. Among them was an opalescent glass bell signed Chance Bros. & Co., Nailsea. This would date the bell between 1810 and 1815, which was when the Chance Brothers managed the Nailsea Glass Works. This is one of the few wedding bells that was signed by a maker.

An unusual wedding bell is one made with cased glass. The one shown herein consists of blue glass with an interior layer of white glass.

A wedding bell that can be readily identified is one that has a pressed glass handle with an impressed English Registry Number. The number permits one to identify which company made the bell, the date when its patent was registered, and the location of the factory.

A close-up of the English Registry Number 176566 on the pressed glass handle.

A blue on white cased glass bell with a three knop clear glass handle. 5"d. x 12-3/4"h. $300-400.

A cranberry glass bell with a "Lemon Pearline" pattern pressed glass handle with opalescent edges. The English Registry Number 176566 on the handle identifies it as having been made by George Davidson & Company, Teams Flint Glass Works, Gateshead-on-Tyne. The pattern was registered on August 15, 1891. 4-1/4"d. x 9"h. $400-500.

American Wedding Bells

Although wedding bells are generally associated with England, there are at least seven companies in the United States and one in France known to have produced wedding type bells.

A pair of cranberry glass bells with an overlay of white glass to form a quilted pattern. The handles are hollow and bulbous with a twisted ribbing pattern and one knop. Based on the shape of the hollow handle and the one knop, the author believes they are American made, possibly Hobbs, Brockunier & Co. Similar bells have sometimes been attributed as early Pairpoint. 6-3/4"d. x 10-1/2"h., c. 1880s. $350-400 ea.

A pair of pattern molded cranberry colored bells with opaque yellow wrythen handles with four knops, blown by J. A. Klumpp for the Thomas Evans Glass Co. 8"d. x 16"h., c. 1898. A similar pair, but larger, is on display at the Corning Museum of Glass, Corning, New York. *Courtesy of Jeremy N. Spear.*

A milk glass bell with tan Nailsea type loops, milk white handle with one knop. Attributed to American glass manufacturer. 7"d. x 10-1/2"h. $300-400.

Four bells possibly attributed to Hobbs, Brockunier & Co. Two bells have a "Coin Spot" pattern, the third has a cranberry swirled design with white rim, and the fourth is milk white with a blue rim. All have bulbous, hollow, two to three knop handles—two clear and two milk white, one of which has multicolored decoration. *Courtesy of the collection of the Museums of Oglebay Institute, Wheeling, WV.*

A dark opaline glass bell with a two knop bulbous hollow handle. Plaster joint is reinforced with a copper ring. 6"d. x 11"h. $300-400.

Wedding Bells Produced in the United States

Company	Location	Dates
Beaumont Glass Company	Martin's Ferry, OH	1895-1901
Hobbs Brockunier & Company	Wheeling, WV	1880-1888
Phoenix Glass Company	Beaver Falls, PA	1832-1868
Portland Glass Company	Portland, ME	1863-1873
Sandwich Coop. Glass Co.	Sandwich, MA	1888-1891
Steuben Glass Works	Corning, NY	1903-1936
Thomas Evans Glass Co.	Pittsburgh, PA	1890s

In the United States, the only glass manufacturer known to have produced glass products in the nineteenth century with mechanical threading is the Boston & Sandwich Co. which produced glass articles with threading of 10 to 12 threads per inch.

A red bell with threading along the lower third and a clear one knop handle. Based on the thread spacing of twelve threads per inch, the author attributes this bell to the Boston and Sandwich Glass Co. 5-3/4"d. x 13-1/2"h. $350-400.

Some of the wedding bells produced by the companies listed in this table are illustrated in Lois Springer's book, *The Collector's Book of Bells*. Additionally, some of the Pairpoint Glass Co. bells shown in Chapter Five can be considered a modern version of a wedding bell.

French Wedding Bells

Among bell collectors there are some wedding bells that have the initials CA on a flat area of the collar where the handle is inserted. These bells are attributed to a French glass company, but the author is not aware of the manufacturer.

Top center: A translucent opaline glass bell with an oval imprint pattern and solid handle with five knops. The collar holding the handle has the initials "CA" on a flat surface, presently attributed to an unknown French company. 6-3/4"d. x 14-3/4"h. $400-450.

Top right: A clear violet bell with diamond quilted pattern and a translucent opaline spire shaped handle. The collar holding the handle has a flat surface with initials "CA," an unknown French glass company. 6-1/4"d. x 15-1/4"h. $500-600.

Right: A clear violet bell with a diamond pattern and dark violet, five knop handle with a twisted ribbing pattern. This bell also has the initials "CA" on a flat portion of the collar holding the handle, attributed to an unknown French company. 6-3/4"d. x 15-1/2"h. $800-900.

References

Boyle, Julia. "Novelties in Glass." *Collectors' Guide.* July 1977: 58, 59.

"Butler Art Museum Wedding Bells." *The Bell Tower Supplement.* June 1970: 5 pages.

Duesselmann, Ethel. "English Glass Bells." *The Bell Tower.* November 1965: 1-7

Mosley, Lillian. "Nailsea Glass." *The Bell Tower.* October 1977: 12-14.

Stacey, Allan. "Coloured Glass Bells." *Antique Collector.* 49, no. 12 (December 1978): 86, 87.

The American Bell Association

The American Bell Association (ABA) is an international association of bell collectors. It was formed originally in 1940 as the National Bell Collectors Club. The name was changed in 1948 to the American Bell Association and the word International added in 1984 to reflect a growing international membership. In 1984, the association was also incorporated as a non-profit organization.

The American Bell Association has forty-five regional, state, Canadian, and overseas chapters that meet on a regular basis. It holds an annual convention during June/July and publishes a bimonthly magazine, *The Bell Tower*, featuring articles by members on all kinds of bells, bell news from around the world, chapter news, and details of important future bell meetings.

Conventions are held in a different location each year and afford members the opportunity to become acquainted with other members and their collections, as well as to forge lasting friendships. Highlights of each convention are a sales room and a bell auction with many opportunities to find bells to add to members' collections.

For further information, write to:

ABA
P. O. Box 19443
Indianapolis, IN 46219

A pair of Fenton bells produced for the American Bell Association to celebrate the new millennium. Left: mold #7650RU, in ruby, 3"d. x 6-3/4"h. Right: oval mold #7650KN, in blue, 2-1/2" x 3-1/2" x 6-1/4"h. Each bell has the American Bell Association logo in gold lettering on one side and "Ringing in the Millennium" on the other. $25-35 ea.

Appendix 2
Cut Glass Patterns

General Bibliography ───────────

Anthony, Dorothy Malone. *The World of Bells.* Des Moines, Iowa: Wallace-Homestead Book
    Co., 1971.
_____. *World of Bells No. 2.* Des Moines, Iowa: Wallace-Homestead Book Co., 1974.
_____. *World of Bells No. 5.* No date.
_____. *Bell Tidings.* No date.
_____. *The Lure of Bells.* 1989.
_____. *World of Collectible Bells.* no date.
_____. *More Bell Lore.* 1993.
_____. *Bells Now and Long Ago.* 1995.
_____. *Legendary Bells.* 1997.
_____. *Bell Treasures.* 1999.
Baker, Donna S. *Collectible Bells: Treasures of Sight and Sound.* Atglen, Pennsylvania: Schiffer
    Publishing Ltd., 1998.
_____. *More Collectible Bells: Classic to Contemporary.* Atglen, Pennsylvania: Schiffer Pub-
    lishing Ltd., 1999.

Index